AND ELSE

AND ELSE

(a version of life according to
MICK STERLING)

– BEAVER'S POND PRESS –

Saint Paul, Minnesota

Praise for *And Else*

"There were times when reading Mick's book that I felt almost indebted to him for taking a turn toward a deeper honesty in place of more familiar platitudes. Other times I was grateful for a unique take on a subject I thought I'd heard enough about. One takes a risk when writing a book this personal. It was well worth the risk."

—TD MISCHKE, *The Mischke Roadshow*

"In the eagle-eyed tradition of finding meaning, madness, and occasional merriment in both life's prosaic and profound realities, Mick Sterling is right up there with Mitch Albom, Dave Barry, and even ol' Erma Bombeck. In these rewarding pages, you'll find a finer appreciation of card tables, toast, loss, the terrors of adolescent swimming, Disney's *Dumbo*, the magic of Bread—the band—and your own life too."

—MARTIN KELLER, author of *Hijinx and Hearsay: Scenester Stories from Minnesota's Pop Life*

"Mick Sterling is a very special guy. You may not notice how special the first time you meet him, or even the second time. But *he* knows exactly how special you are after he meets *you*. Now you can find out just how special he really is after you read his engaging book of essays, *And Else*.

Discover a talented musician and songwriter, singer, philanthropist, father, husband, and a very humorous and thoughtful soul (who even played on the same stage as Prince Rogers Nelson). In this book, you'll learn a lot about Mick—like why he thinks it's not right to have to swim naked in gym class (I swear)! Or why card tables are so important. As you'll see in *And Else*, he knows what's important in LIFE, including music, art, respect, faith, heartbreak, and humor. But most of all you'll wish Mick was your friend, brother, and maybe even your Papa."

—LOUIE ANDERSON, Emmy Award-winning actor, comedian, bestselling author, and St. Paul native

Also by Mick Sterling

The Long Ride Home

One hundred percent of the proceeds from *And Else* will be set aside to raise funds for these two charitable efforts:

1. The 30-Days Foundation, www.The30-DaysFoundation.org. The 30-Days Foundation assists individuals and families living in Minnesota who are in real-life financial crisis, with a one-time financial grant that is only made payable to the service provider that requires payment.

2. The Masterpiece Foundation Grant. This is a partnership between Mick Sterling Presents and the Angel Foundation in the Twin Cities to honor the life and work of Tucker Sterling Jensen. Funds donated to the Angel Foundation will be set aside for The Masterpiece Foundation Grant requests. These grants will allow people who are dealing with cancer to continue to create their legacy throughout their treatment. Donations will assist with hotel stays, fuel costs, tuition needs, and funding to help them continue their efforts to create a better life for themselves, and their families, during this stressful time.

This is a work of creative nonfiction. The events are portrayed to the best of Mick Sterling's memory.

Edited by Kerry Jade Aberman
Production editor: Hanna Kjeldbjerg
Cover photo by Peter Guertin
Author photo by Peter Guertin

Photos on pages 6 and 24 by Lotus Productions.
Photos on pages 12 and 142 by Jensen Family Photo.
Photo on page 18 by Jessica Katherine Jensen Dixon.
Photo on page 30 by Scott Sansby.
Photo on page 40 by Charlie Peterson.
Photo on page 48 by Gary Eckhart.
Photos on pages 76 and 136 by Neil Schloner.
Photos on pages 84, 164, and 206 by Peter Guertin.
Photo on page 92 by Bayfront Blues Fest.
Photos on pages 98, 172, and 182 by Kathleen Tauer.
Photo on page 111 by Mick Sterling.
Photos on pages 118 and 130 by Jim Vasquez.
Photos on pages 148 and 194 by Mikaela Jensen.
Photo on page 188 by Deb Runkle.
All other photo credits unknown.

ISBN 13: 978-1-64343-843-6
Library of Congress Catalog Number: 2020923868
Printed in the United States of America
First Printing: 2021
25 24 23 22 21   5 4 3 2 1

Book design and typesetting by Athena Currier.

 Pond Reads Press
939 Seventh Street West, Saint Paul, MN 55102
(952) 829-8818 | www.BeaversPondPress.com

To order, visit www.MickSterlingPresents.com. Reseller discounts available.

Contact Mick Sterling at www.MickSterlingPresents.com for speaking engagements, book club discussions, freelance writing projects, and interviews.

Every day, flashes and glimpses happen
in a wonderful adventure ahead.

—143

I'm glad I've failed. It's proof I put it out there.

—MICK STERLING

Contents

Foreword

It's Sunday, March 22, 2020, in Minneapolis.

We are potentially hours or, at best, days away from being in a complete city lockdown because of COVID-19.

My mother was always on the go. I'm just like her. For me, not having a place to go, whether to work, to drive to, or just to feel I've accomplished something, isn't good. Being in shutdown takes a toll on me, and on anyone around me.

At this current time, there are all kind of scary scenarios about this virus. There are some people who are facing this news with dread. Some are suspicious of the seed: Why is all of this happening to us, and where did the virus come from? Some fear for civilization in general.

I find myself grouchy at the diminished opportunity to do what I do in the time given to me. I am fully aware of the magnitude of what is happening, and I'm adjusting everything, as everyone else is, to fit into the parameters of what this is, and what it could be. But I'm still upset with it.

I have to do what I can while I can, and dammit, I'm going to do it. I'm doing everything I can to stay positive. That's another reason why I'm starting this book.

A few years ago, my first book, *The Long Ride Home*, was published by a very kind man named Dāv Kaufman. For a while, he had a publishing company called Crotalus Publishing.

Of all my life's artistic accomplishments, having my own book published was the thing I could never have imagined would happen. It was a thrill.

However, it was not a financial bonanza for my friend, and it certainly didn't help that the band I was most known for was, for all the reasons everyone has heard a thousand times before, soon to break up.

But saying that, let me just clarify this: we didn't break up because of a love triangle, or a love rectangle, or because one of the band members wasn't contributing to the rent of the band house. It was just time to stop for a while. We did, and now we're back performing, and it's more beautiful than ever, thankfully.

I am fully aware there is no real reason to write this book, and it could not be any more presumptuous to believe that anyone will focus any time on any of my ramblings.

There are millions of books for people to read. Why mine? Why, indeed?

I wish this narrative were derived from an author who endured an *Angela's Ashes* type of childhood, and who bears the scars of that experience. But, it is not.

I was raised in Crystal, Minnesota. I went to school in the Robbinsdale School District 281 in the 1960s and 1970s, and everything was completely fine. I had plenty of Wonder Bread, mixing-bowl-sized portions of cereal, sixteen-ounce ice-cold Coca-Colas I could down anytime, and a badass stereo I annoyed my neighborhood with because I played it too loud. I was just fine, thank you very much.

In 2020, I will enter my fifty-ninth year, and my motivation, professionally, is to not say 'no' to anything within my ability to attempt. Why the hell not?

What follows are new, and older, observations of life, and how I view it. These include observations from my personal and professional life, and those issued as columns on social media platforms, from Myspace through Facebook.

They also include tidbit observations and comments I made on Facebook, that glorified Lite-Brite, just to create a break from the platform's stream of angst and hyperbole.

I find I have a fascination for confounding people who see me as they see me.

I like doing different things.

I don't like failing, but I'm glad I have failed. It means I've made the effort to try something new, instead of settling for not trying because something was scary. Failure makes the victories more memorable.

4

mick sterling

I have had some success, but I am completely aware that I am one penny in a jar, and while the level of my worth is exactly the same as every other penny, I am a penny in a place where only quarters and silver dollars get noticed. Alas, that is my lot in the music business in the Twin Cities. I'm a penny in a professional music jar, and for me, that puts me in the game and I'm grateful.

This book is called *And Else*. That is not a word you'll find in any dictionary.

But my son, Tucker, used this word when he was a little boy. He used that word when he was explaining something to me and needed to add one more thing to the content of his story. An example would be, "Papa, I want to watch *Sonic the Hedgehog* for a while, andelse after that, let's watch *Gargoyles*."

I liked the word. I knew what he meant when he said it, and that's good enough for me.

I know there is no reason for this book, andelse, I hope you enjoy it.

I think we all better be more worried about the popularity of The Masked Singer than we are. I'm not kidding.

The Conquering of "Hot Cross Buns"

There is a spark in every established musician, whether he is a professional musician, the guitar god or Lizard King of his basement, or the bonfire/campfire guitarist who starts the sing-along on the pontoon boat each summer.

As large a spark as it is, it's surprising how few musicians, if any, actually remember this particular spark.

Perhaps they do not remember because the moment of the spark was not one that could be seen or heard. It was not something placed in front of them. It's normally something so deep and natural to them that it's as commonplace as inhaling and exhaling. The only thing that differentiates this spark from the simple act of taking breath is that this spark makes every breath, once embraced and accepted, a kind of compass that guides their movements for everything that follows. Once this spark is ignited, the momentum with which a learning musician plays their instrument depends on many things.

Some of it depends upon how adept the person is at the chosen instrument, whether there's a natural affinity for the instrument, you could say. Some of it will be tied to how much time they spend on the instrument, how much they practice, etc. There are some people who can just pick something up and play it naturally.

But no matter what level they reach, every musician eventually learns their instrument enough to feel like a musician, and every musician is united by one thing . . . there was a time when every one of them had no idea how to play the instrument of their choosing. At one time, when they held that instrument, they didn't have a clue as to what to do with it. Everyone has to learn. Everyone has to pick up that instrument for the first time and accept the fact that they are clueless, until they start that long process of learning the instrument. Everyone begins somewhere.

While each instrument is different and has its own unique sound and soul, there seems to be one song that, once conquered, is the springboard to hundreds, if not thousands, of other songs.

I'm talking of course of the "Brown Eyed Girl" and "Sweet Caroline" of many beginning musicians, the musical Mount Everest that must, and fortunately can, be climbed, if a musician is to stand any chance of continuing their love affair with their instrument. First, they must learn and play the song called "Hot Cross Buns." "Hot Cross Buns"—I've always been fascinated by the song. Why is it called "Hot Cross Buns"?

Why is this song used as the song that beginners must learn? There must be other simple songs out there. And perhaps there are, but they certainly aren't as popular, or as fun to say, as "Hot Cross Buns."

Who wrote "Hot Cross Buns"? Is this mysterious person getting royalties each time the song is performed or written? Does the writer of "Hot Cross Buns" live like Howard Hughes in silent solitude, or does he own the entire Eastern Seaboard from all the money he has made from this oft-performed chestnut? I'm confident I'll never know the answer, but what I do know is the conquering of "Hot Cross Buns" is a milestone for any musician who learns it.

It's validation you chose the right instrument. It's validation you can learn if you put time into this instrument. It's validation that the spark that ignited something inside you to take up this instrument was the right choice. It's validation of being one step closer to how your imagination depicts you playing this instrument, with a fluidity and expertise that your current reality does not provide. Conquering this song is confirmation to any musician that he or she can take on what's next. This simple song is powerful, and will continue to be powerful, as long as there are young boys and girls who are searching for that place in their soul that is yearning for something more, something that cannot be provided by friendship, faith, popularity, wealth, comfort, love, or hate.

While it's true someone else can purchase the instrument and the sheet music to "Hot Cross Buns" to get you going, you can't purchase something that's not for sale. The spark to learn your instrument cannot be bought; it can only be identified and acted upon. So applaud, and applaud loudly, when your child accomplishes "Hot Cross Buns," because what follows will stimulate their soul and mold them into the person they will become.

This is what I want. I want to smell like cookies. That's all I want.

The Stillness of Christmas

Stillness can take many forms. One kind of stillness, a flurry of turmoil and sadness about this time of year, can render some people to be pushed into a darker corner than usual. The feeling of not being good enough, of not doing enough for yourself and for others, of not being able to take care of your family the way you want to, of being unfulfilled personally and professionally, and dozens of other scenarios, can level you.

It's as if, for some people, this time of year holds a magnifying glass over them twenty-four hours a day. It is like a stick poking and prodding them, or a knife, dissecting them and the secrets and fears they've been able to hide from others throughout the other eleven months of the year. But now, not so much.

This kind of stillness can grip and guide a person to places they know they shouldn't go. Yet they feel compelled to go, as punishment, for feeling the way they do during this time of year. This is one of the elements of the season that is so disheartening for me to see others experience.

We can be very hard on ourselves at this time of the year. Too hard. I'm not sure this heightened level of self-execution is worth all the anguish. The majority of the time, it doesn't solve much more than if we didn't experience this anguish in the first place.

After all, it's a season of spiritual and cultural significance, and God certainly knew what He was doing when He invented a thing called "the next day."

Nobody knows what will happen the next day. As much as we think we do, we don't; and as much as we think we're intelligent enough to assume and deduce, we aren't. How can we anguish over something when we have no idea what it will be? Or who it is? Or where it will come from?

While this season can certainly inspire sadness, uncertainty can also inspire wonder.

There is a stillness that I feel during Christmas, at times of anticipation. It is not the same anticipation I had as a child, when I'd wonder how many Hot Wheels cars I'd get and the amount of track I would receive to set up around my house. It is the anticipation of what's next from what I've lived this year.

What did I learn? What will I learn in the future from what I've experienced?

Were my actions and words inspired by compassion and creativity, or at times did they fall flat because I wasn't focused and secure enough in the execution of them?

Is what I'm doing making a difference in the lives of the people I love as well as to people I don't even know? As I grow older and more confident in many aspects of my own being, I have come to love the anticipation of not being sure of anything, even professionally, despite my growing confidence in other aspects of life. I guess it's like being grateful for the nervousness that comes when I'm in a performance situation that is beyond my comfort zone. My nervousness reminds me that I still care, and that I have a healthy level of respect for my craft.

There is a stillness that will present itself to me on Christmas Eve. It was there when I was a child, and it continues to this day.

As the sun sets on Christmas Eve, and the cover of night descends upon us all, I can feel a collective sigh around us, a deep breath that we all seem to breathe at relatively the same time. It binds us, and nudges us, and coaxes us to slow down.

The last-minute shoppers at the mall and grocery stores are heading home. The employees, grateful to be done with their shifts, are now home. The streets seem lonelier, and somehow, grateful for the peace and quiet. The stoplights seem kinder, with more green lights greeting your presence, guiding you back safely to your home. People are showering, bathing, resting, doing whatever is needed before bedtime with the family. They get in their cars knowing they've done all they can do to prepare, and now it's time to experience what they've spent so much time, energy, and money on.

Judgment will be declared about their efforts when the presents purchased are greeted with cheer or apathy. Guards will hopefully be let down when family is together. Drinking wine, eating a good dinner, and reminiscing about an array of joyful, sorrowful, and embarrassing moments will hopefully bring the appropriate emotions and responses, keeping the gathering on a heartfelt path. It is these kinds of activities, within the stillness of the season, that provide a hopefully clearer, more optimistic vision of what was, and what's potentially to be.

There are loved ones we will miss this season. There are enemies and people who have hurt others so deeply that while they stand a chance of being forgiven, they most likely won't be. There will be yearnings for things to improve for loved ones, for circumstances to become better than what they are experiencing now.

There will be awakenings of feelings thought to be buried. There will be wonder in the eyes of a child truly enjoying a present—and there will be a deeper level of love than a parent ever thought they could experience, as they watch their child experience what they had once felt when they were their kid's age.

There will be the wisdom of grandparents, who continue to act surprised when things happen to their older children, despite having lived and seen the whole movie before. In short, life will happen before us. I wish for all of you your own stillness. Not a stillness of atrophy, or fear, or dread, but a stillness of knowing there is more love in this world than hate.

There is more humor around you, and in you, than you may know. And you should notice it and embrace it. I wish for all of you the stillness of knowing that, should you choose to view it this way, ignorance of what's ahead can be a blessing instead of a burden. I wish for all of you the stillness that gives you strength and hope this season and, more importantly, every day of every year. I wish for all of you a wonderful holiday, however you celebrate it. We made it through, didn't we?

That's something to be thankful for.

I know I am.

Grandmas, we need those five-dollar bills more than ever. Keep 'em comin!

Mom's Bed

This is a complicated and turbulent world we are all experiencing. While it cannot be denied that life can be hard in America during these tough economic times, it's important to remember that there are people living today who are far worse off economically, politically, and physically.

They don't have the smallest percentage of the blessings and comforts that even someone living beneath the poverty line in America has. That is not to lessen the pain and anguish that comes along with minute-by-minute knowledge of struggling to put food on the table for one's family, but it's also a fact that there are people in this world who are far worse off than us. We are each unique in our own way, but we are all human, and our bodies are remarkably similar underneath the given color of our skin.

We also all come from a female, who is given a new name and duty once a new life is inside her.

Our experiences, as our fingerprints, are our own, and thankfully they can't be duplicated. Who molds us as our parental figures, whether they are our actual parents, or family, or friends who are adults and take on that role, of course plays a huge role in how we all turn out.

There are multiple reasons in all of us defining our uniqueness. But perhaps there is one thing that binds us in some way.

One thing that lies so deep within us that when, as adults, we are nudged toward it by proximity or recollection, it can transport us to a place long-closed by age.

A place of complete safety and warmth. A place where the world, which at times felt scary and burdensome because of your own shyness, or awkwardness, or loneliness as a child, embraced you and reminded you where your real home was.

There is only one place that can wear that title, and it just may be the one common denominator for the vast majority of people from countries all around the world . . . That place is Mom's Bed.

Mom's Bed.

The bed that she lay in when you were inside her, when you were no bigger than a speck, when she found out something was going on inside her that was going to change everything.

The same bed she shared with either her boyfriend or husband, having late-night discussions about who would do what when the baby came and brought with it thousands of plans, plans they had no real clue how to manage, plans they would figure out somehow.

Or perhaps it is the bed your mother cried herself to sleep in, because she was so afraid of how she alone was going to raise this life growing inside her.

Mom's Bed.

The bed where, while you were still inside, you kicked her so hard, and often, that you wouldn't allow her to sleep. The bed where a voice sang and spoke to you multiple times a day, before you even entered this world. The bed where you were breastfed, or given a bottle multiple times each day, while you looked up at her smiling, reassuring face.

The bed where, nightly, the same voice sang you to sleep, or pled with you to stop crying long enough so she could sleep for at least a few minutes before she had to wake again. The bed that was your ultimate goal to get back into when your mother or father finally placed you in your own bed, and made you sleep the whole night in your own room. The bed that was your safe haven when ugly ghosts, wind monsters, curious owls, or angry giraffes peeking through your window scared you enough that you jumped out of your bed.

Mom's Bed.

The bed with the nightstand, and the purse that had every conceivable remedy to whatever ailed you, all within reach of your mother, to help you when you were hurting or sad. The bed that smelled of her perfume and that one lotion she always used, the scent of a world that you and you alone really knew, because it felt like a world created specifically for you.

Mom's Bed.

As you got older, it was Mom's Bed that was still a place of comfort and safety, the place to really cry and cry hard if you hurt yourself. The place you could let go, in a way you couldn't in front of your friends.

It was the bed where you could flop with your feet hanging off the side and tell your mom what happened that day, who was mean to whom, which boys or girls you had a crush on, what happened in school, your dreams, your fears, and any other thing that crossed your mind.

It was the bed that was truly the only place you could really take a good, strong, long nap, because once you settled in, it was unlike your bed, or any other bed. Because, well . . . it was Mom's Bed.

Mom's Bed.

Every parent has a thousand responsibilities in taking care of their own child or children. Any parent would gladly take a few minutes to slip away, to regain the sense of comfort they felt when they had no responsibility, except to be around, to be loved by their own mom.

Mom's Bed.

Most of the time, unlike your bed, Mom's Bed was made, perfect, and inviting. The blankets were perfect. Only moms have that ability.

It's too bad we can't all just lay in that bed, to gather ourselves a bit from time to time. Perhaps, if we could, things wouldn't be so tough, and mean people wouldn't be so mean.

I have invested ten thousand dollars into a new company that that has created a hemp and craft beer bitcoin pre-natal education experience for new parents. I foresee big things developing.

The Walking Helmet

INVESTMENT PROPOSAL #2954567

NAME OF PRODUCT: Walking Helmet

PROPOSED BY: Mick Sterling

REASON FOR PROPOSAL: The safety of mankind, as observed by an extremely athletic and poised person (myself) tripping. IT MUST BE STOPPED!

LOCATION OF PROPOSAL: United States of America

WHERE PRODUCT WILL BE ACCESSED: Worldwide

WHEN PRODUCT WILL BE ACCESSED: As soon as humanly possible because people are hurting themselves and/or dying

PRICE POINT OF PRODUCT: $74.99

LOCATION OF PRODUCT SALES: Sam's Club, Walmart, Target, Mills' Fleet Farm, all Walgreens locations, all superettes, gas stations, ice cream trucks, hot dog stands, baseball stadiums, football stadiums, soccer stadiums, anywhere people stand upright and decide on a whim to move in a forward, or backward, motion

MANUFACTURING OF PRODUCT: Anywhere except the United States of America

WHO WOULD PURCHASE THIS PRODUCT: All citizens of the world who inhale and/or exhale

WHY THIS PRODUCT IS NEEDED NOW: This is the most dangerous time in human history. There have never been more obstacles for us to overcome, especially as Americans, than right now. The Great Depression, World War I and II, The Dustbowl, The Civil War, The War of 1812, The Revolutionary War, and other instances of pain in America pale in comparison to what all of us are going through right now. Because of that, this product is needed now more than ever.

HOW THE PRODUCT WORKS: The customer will be able to live their life in a more secure, fashionable, and socially-acceptable way with the Walking Helmet. Not only will the Walking

Helmet protect the most important commodity in our society, our children, it will protect all humans of all ages.

WHAT YOU CAN DO WHILE WEARING THE PRODUCT:

- You can walk downhill, or uphill, without fear.

- You can reach for things on the ground without fear of falling on your face and cracking your skull.

- Worries about cracking your head on the headboard during sexual intercourse are all but eradicated if you wear the Walking Helmet during sex.

- The inventors recommend wearing Walking Helmets on all merry-go-rounds, running tracks, hamster wheels, and, of course, when ordering and consuming ice cream.

LIFESTYLE: The Walking Helmet can be worn as you live life vertically or horizontally. It can be worn inside your home, or outside in the general public. Any design you wish may be placed upon the Walking Helmet, but it must have a license number in clear sight, ensuring you can be seen up close and from the safety-observation satellites stationed at various intervals around the rings of Saturn.

HOW TO WEAR THE PRODUCT: The Walking Helmet can be manually placed on the head by the consumer in two ways: place securely on head and secure the Velcro straps around chin, or, for an additional $24.99, the consumer can purchase the Walking Helmet Skull Cap.

The WH Skull Cap fits securely around the head and is filled with magnetic patches to secure your Walking Helmet in an even safer way. As safe as these options are, the inventors of the Walking Helmet recommend the customer purchases the "Will" Permit for an additional $49.99 for the safest method of living with the Walking Helmet.

This permit, once purchased, will direct or "will" the Walking Helmet to secure itself to the head automatically. The consumer will never have to reach for their Walking Helmet. The Walking Helmet will sense your presence, in or out of the home, and place itself near you.

When you decide to move in any direction from a seated or horizontal position, the Walking Helmet with the purchased permit will automatically secure itself on your head. This saves precious energy by storing the energy you may have used when employing your arms, elbows, hands, and fingers to place and secure the Walking Helmet on your head.

10-YEAR GOAL: For every human and pet to feel uncomfortable moving without the Walking Helmet.

The inventors estimate that 2.5 million lives will be saved each month by wearing the Walking Helmet.

INVESTMENT SOUGHT TO BRING PRODUCT TO MARKET:
$2.5 Trillion Dollars and 4 Goats

RETURN TO INVESTOR: The peace of mind of knowing you are protecting people's heads

Thank you for your time and consideration.

Mick Sterling
Esquire

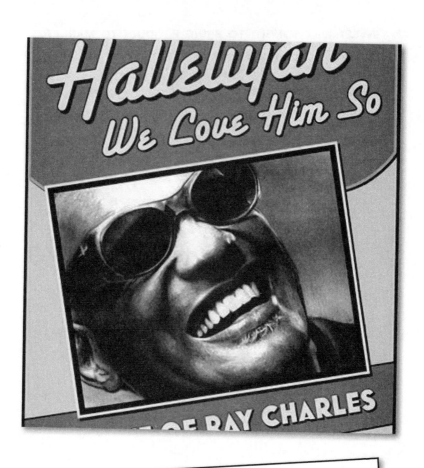

The guitar that Prince threw up in the air at the Rock and Roll Hall of Fame performance of "While My Guitar Gently Weeps" just fell on my head at Cracker Barrel today. Anything is possible kids, don't give up!

That One Night

The first two recordings I was ever involved in were at a studio in the Uptown area of Minneapolis. The studio was called Moon Sound Studios. It was run by a gentleman named Chris Moon.

I was a kid who loved listening to the full albums of people who influenced me. I was just getting my feet wet playing in a band. These were my pre-songwriting days, so a chance to go into a studio was quite thrilling.

The first song my friend Peter Guertin and I ever went into a studio to record was this old Elton John song called "Rock Me When He's Gone." Long John Baldry had recorded it first. We did it with our bandmates, John Rochon and Jeff Swagger, and as I'm writing this, I can't for the life of me remember why we did it, but I'm glad we did. Hearing us in headphones, standing in a studio singing, was something that I thought would never happen. It was very dreamlike, actually.

The second time we went to Moon Sound was with a cast of friends, and we recorded songs for the *Godspell* show we self-produced one summer. As we slayed the songs from *Godspell* like no one's business, we were told we were the first project to get into Moon Sound since a young man by the name of Prince Rogers Nelson had finished recording.

They shared with us that this young man was in the studio constantly. He was so committed to what he was doing, he actually slept in the studio at times. He wrote all of his own songs, and he played every instrument on the recording. That blew our minds. How can anyone do that? I knew at the time Stevie Wonder did that, but Stevie Wonder wasn't from Minneapolis, nor had Stevie Wonder just been in the studio I was in. So, yes, my mind was blown indeed.

That young man released his first album, and everyone knows the rest of the story about his remarkable life, and his outstandingly diverse catalog of music, which while borrowing from many genres, stood alone. He created his own genre, and artists will draw upon it for decades.

Prince passed away just a few weeks after I did a show at the Fireside Theatre inside the Chanhassen Dinner Theatres. Something inconceivable had happened that night. Prince joined us on stage.

What follows is my testimony of that night in 2016. It was picked up by the *Star Tribune* and went viral.

REMEMBERING PRINCE:
HIS MUSIC, OUR MOMENTS

By Mick Sterling

The outpouring of love and devotion to Prince Rogers Nelson is inspiring and awesome.

Everyone has their own Prince story, either as a fan or a musician.

A huge calling card for any musician is to say that he "played with Prince" at one time or another. My message, in that column, was to tell you this: we all played with Prince, and he let us play with him.

We did.

And it was a wondrous thing for all involved. We are all damned fortunate it happened in our lifetime. Recently, I had the good fortune to, as they say in show business, "share the stage" with Prince. This phrase is a very loose term for bands and artists like me, who have lived their lives in clubland and local festivals.

To say you "shared the stage" with a national artist, for example, could be ethically and logistically defined as you having played on the same stage as the national artist, even if you were the opening act of a thirteen-hour music festival, and they headlined. And believe me, the phrase has been used for decades as a selling tool for local artists, and it will continue to be used, despite it not being exactly accurate.

This particular evening in Chanhassen, however, "sharing the stage" really came true for the incredible band I led, and the remarkably fortunate 240 people in the room to witness it. We were doing a Ray Charles show. And what happened in that room that night was, to me, quintessentially Minneapolis.

Prince knew some people in the band that night. Perhaps that's why he felt comfortable coming to this particular show. I had never met Prince prior, and despite people thinking we met and talked that night, the truth is, I never met him that night either.

Our eyes met on stage when he decided to join us for the one minute he was up there. My job, as the leader of the band, was to let it happen, and to watch his eyes. Because the moment I saw him look at me, or Bobby Vandell (who was playing drums during Prince's solo), that would be my cue to start singing again. When he did, I started singing.

Prince gave the guitar back to Stephen Morgan, our guitar player, and he walked off the stage. To the stunned amazement and joy of the audience and

band, Prince left the stage as quickly and freely as he'd
appeared.

That night was an organic and lovely Minneapolis
music moment that we were all blessed to witness.
There were lots of smiles and good vibes. There is no
way to downplay that moment; it was beyond thrilling. Today, that moment is sweeter and sadder than
it has ever been.

The international fame of Prince is the direct
opposite of the intimate relationship you feel with
him, or with any artist, for that matter, who has
moved you.

While the entire world has access to the inter-
net, and to the technology that plays his CDs, tapes,
albums, and even eight-tracks, all of us have also had
that special moment with him that is uniquely ours
and ours alone.

Who hasn't sung in their car to Prince? Or
danced in their underwear, alone in their room, playing air guitar to Prince's amazing solos and lip-synch-
ing "Darling Nikki" to the mirror? Perhaps you've
lain on your bed listening to *1999*, *Lovesexy*, *Purple
Rain*, *Sign o' the Times*, *Controversy*, or any of the other
albums that moved you and that you let soak in at
that age. Those were your times.

Time alone with Prince that no one can take from you. No one experienced what you experienced with Prince. That is alone time, uniquely yours, with a genius. This is one of the many reasons his passing cuts us so deeply to the core.

I have been blessed to have performed with many people who played with Prince in Minneapolis. They are better people and better musicians for it. What a remarkable connection to have.

Whether they knew Prince when he was starting out, living in North Minneapolis and playing at the Capri Theater on West Broadway, or a few years later, when he was just taking off, we can only imagine what that must have felt like, to be around someone with that talent and creativity. And while stories abound of how difficult it was, at times, to work with Prince, I categorize those as the "omelette / broken eggs" syndrome.

When you work with someone that brilliant, who knows what they want, and has the ability to actually realize it, at times, it's going to be unpleasant. Because you can't match the intensity of someone who knows what they want and is driven to make it happen, because it's absolutely what *must* happen. Musicians who played with Prince have most likely seen that side of him at times.

But I also hear, an overwhelming amount of the time, working with Prince was a surreal, intense, and beautiful thing that musicians felt blessed to be a part of, because they truly were.

What we are finding out about this talented man since his passing is that countless times he provided people with unheralded and unadvertised philanthropy. His outreach to those in need was something nobody, apart from his innermost circle, knew of. His innate need to do for others is something to be admired.

He was a human being with feelings, and at times, he was hurt by the hurtful things said about him. Things you didn't think he knew about, but he did. He was a man. An extremely gifted man, but a man nonetheless.

We are also hearing all kinds of things about how he passed. Some of the rumors are ugly. I am choosing to ignore those. I know how he lived, and that was stunning. How he passed is private and, quite frankly, none of our business. I don't want to know that about Prince, or about anybody famous. Unless I'm related to the person, why do I really need to know?

Here's what I do know: the *Lovesexy* show at Met Center made me want to stop playing. I figured what's the point, really. It was the greatest concert and spectacle I have, to this day, ever seen. I said that night, and still believe, it just couldn't get better than that. For any mere mortal, it couldn't. But for Prince, it most assuredly did, thousands of times.

He was the ultimate badass. Every musician of every genre had to step back and give it to him. And I, for one minute, was lucky enough to be close to him on stage. I actually, *officially*, shared the stage with Prince. Every day I think of it; it's pretty damned cool.

Yesterday we lost a friend everybody knew, but nobody knew like you did, and it hurts. It hurts like hell.

Thank you, Prince. Thanks for giving us what you did in the time provided to you. Someone like you will not happen to us again. The music world ain't like it was when you arrived on the scene, and it never will be again.

All we can do now is listen, remember, and recollect the beauty and wonder within you, which you gave to all of us.

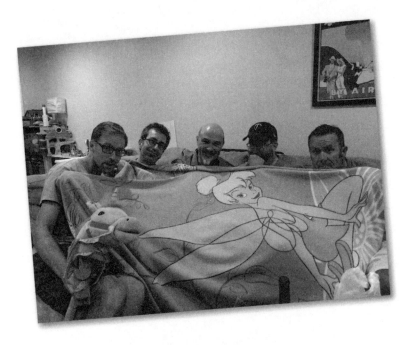

Words mean things. And
so do your loved ones.

You're Like Family to Me

In my late teens, my mother and father remarried after being divorced for nearly fifteen years.

Between that time when I was quite young, my father fell in love and married a woman named Katherine. Katherine was a lovely woman inside and out, and our family loved her very much.

Katherine gave birth to a beautiful child named Jessica, who was my fourth sister. As a twelve-year-old boy, taking care of the baby version of Jessica gave me a great spring training to go through before I'd get the chance to take care of Tucker and Mikaela later in life.

Katherine tragically passed away at a very early age, leaving Jessica without a mother before she was three years old. Her passing was a huge loss to us.

I have so many fond memories of Katherine, whom we called Kitty. She was such a lovely stepmom, and she was so much fun. Her passing marked the first person I loved who died.

Her wake, my first wake, was the first time I ever saw a lifeless body. It was at that moment I realized what a soul was. I realized, looking at Kitty in her casket, that she was nowhere near being there anymore. She was a shell. Kitty was not there. Later that night, it comforted me greatly to know she wasn't there; she did not see everyone sad around her. That was big stuff for a young boy to realize. I'm forever grateful I did discover that.

My father remarried again and it ended badly.

Eventually, my father and mother decided to give marriage to each other another try. It was a mistake from the start.

I know as an author I have the ability, and perhaps duty, to elaborate on all of these rather substantial moments, but these are personal things within my family, and I'm not sure they're shareable to non-family members, or even close friends. Needless to say, there was significant sadness, pain, shame, and a few other particularly unpleasant things that we all went through.

Let's keep going.

The last years of my father's life were filled with pain and horrible decisions, driven by alcohol, and a seemingly constant, disturbing theme of his own family, which flowed through him like poison.

When my father passed, we were not in a good place with each other, and, in fact, I had no idea where he even was. Yet, the moment I found out, I forgave him. Because everything he did, for some odd reason, had a motivation behind it.

My father's life seemed to have been dictated from the atmosphere he came from. His father disciplined and dictated his will upon him. His mother, being a woman of the time, most likely had to sit quietly and endure whatever was spewing from her husband's mouth to their three sons. His voice was likely the law in their house.

It seemed that everything my father was, everything he tried to be, and his failures, were all set in motion by what he went through with a group of people called family, people he had to live with, having no choice in the matter whatsoever.

As I started my own family, I was keenly aware that despite the issues my father displayed to me, my sisters, and my mom, I was ultimately in control of my own trajectory. I was not beholden to repeat what I had seen in my own childhood.

I was also aware that what I had experienced was not one-tenth of what my older sisters went through with my father, and I was grateful my little sister didn't have to experience the years of hardship with him that my older sisters went through. Although she certainly had her moments with our father, similar to my knowledge that my father loved me, I am confident that my father loved Jessica.

I don't want this to lead anyone into thinking my childhood was terrible, because it wasn't. My mother loved me very much. My father, too, loved me very much; he did the best he could. There are multiple things he did that were baffling and painful to witness and experience, but that's the father I had.

My family is lovely. I wish some things hadn't happened in my life, and I wish there were some things I didn't witness. But who can't make that claim?

Everyone has friends and family members. As a child, the composition of your family is beyond your control.

As a parent, you did play a role in the decision of your family, because your heart chose the person you started your family with.

The decision of friendship is also an effort, where your gut decides more often than your heart whether that person will remain a friend to you temporarily, or for the rest of your life.

Both friends and family mold the person you are each day. Both certainly played an important role in defining you.

As we get older, nearly all of us meet multiple people who play important roles in deciding who we are and what we do. These people can, at times, be elevated to the category of "family," even if they aren't sharing the same blood or legal bounds of marriage and adoption.

When people reach that level of closeness with someone, it seems natural to consider them a family member, despite it not being legal.

After all, if it's in your heart, what does it matter if it's legal or not, or if blood is shared between you both? You feel what you feel, and they feel what they feel. It is your relationship, between you and that person who is close to you, and that's all that really matters in the end.

What is interesting to me, though, is the question of importance and priority when those you love and respect are considered actual family members. Is an actual family member, whom you had no choice in having, more important than the wished-upon-and-chosen family member?

Ask any brother or sister about their siblings, and they will say their siblings are the only people who knew them and watched them develop, right from the beginning. Siblings know the real truth behind the stories that have been slowly and methodically embellished, or unconsciously diminished.

Older siblings know of how younger siblings were when they were in diapers and learning how to eat, talk, and walk. They know how you did in school, how your parents dealt with you, your first love, whether you had acne, when you got your period, experienced your first heartbreak, the mistakes you made, and more, as you grew up. They know all of these things because they witnessed them, living in the same home as you. These are things you can only share in words to those close enough to you to be considered honorary family members later in your life.

The friends you consider family have found a version of you that was crafted by the people in your original family, for both bad and good.

Hopefully when they found that version of you, they found a version that was molded by a happy and nurturing home.

But I find that the majority of the time when someone calls a friend their "family," it's because they wish the chosen family member were in their real family.

They wish that person had been around in the terrible, awkward, and painful moments they had as a child with their immediate family, so that their life could have been easier during that time. Perhaps that chosen family member really would have made it easier, but it's pure speculation.

It is certainly understandable though. Who wouldn't want some relief from a friend during all the turmoil of those developing years? It would be wonderful to go back in time and have the friend you have now actually *be* a family member during that same time frame. How much better would your life have been if that could have been true? It's a lovely image to have in your head; but factually, and as the rules of ancestry dictate, that is all it can be: an image.

You can't place people from your present into your past. All you can control is how you present yourself now as a representative of the family that you came from. Your blood and/or legal family is the one that knew you when you were a piece of clay, not yet remotely formed into the person you are today.

When people who are so important to us we consider them family come into our lives, both sides are blessed. As you get older, it is perfectly within your right to choose people that touch your heart and to consider them your family members. Count yourself lucky to have people in your life that give you such comfort and contentment and show you that kind of love. It doesn't happen to everyone.

As special as those people are, though, they are only in that position now because of the family members you didn't choose back then. That is the family that provided you with the desire to let in these special people you met later in life, to fill some void of yours.

The family members you didn't choose are the ones who saw you learn, love, make mistakes, scramble, fumble, throw tantrums, and do stupid and brilliant things. They know you as only they can. They, and they alone, are your family.

You may have multiple families in your life, but only one will be your first family. And this "unchosen" family can't help but play a role in who you are today. It doesn't completely define you, but at a minimum, it provides the blueprint of the structure of your life. It guides your decisions. You can let that first family define you, but as important as your family is, it doesn't get the permission to define you unless you give it that permission.

You define you. You define yourself every day.

Your family is in the mix of that definition of yourself, but in the end, it's up to you.

It is.

You could, if you feel strong enough, make your masterpiece.

We Lost Our Boy

We lost Tucker on March 11th, 2019.

As unique and awful as losing Tucker was for me, his mama, sister, close friends, and the music peers he encouraged and influenced, what transpired during his illness and lasted through his final weeks, days, and hours of life, was so sadly beautiful to me.

That fact never leaves me. It gives me tremendous peace. Not complete peace, mind you; we'll never have that. But some peace in the room, and that's a blessing worth acknowledging.

The closest description I can give to people who ask me how it feels to lose a child is this: your sense of taste changes forever.

Everything tastes different after losing a child. It's not that food tastes bad if you eat it, and you know you have to eat it, but it's just not the same.

I am adapting, because I have to adapt to how things taste now. And I will. But denying that everything in life tastes different is unrealistic. And if you're not careful, everything in your life atrophies.

Tucker Sterling Jensen was born on September 24th, 1989.

Every baby that is born is beautiful. So was Tucker. Tucker was extraordinarily beautiful.

There are a thousand Tucker stories that could be told, and when told properly, they are very, very entertaining.

My earliest relationship with Tucker, when he was a baby, was one of tension and frustration, despite him being so damned cute.

He just did not want me to hold him for any length of time. He wanted his mama, and I understood that, but I remember Tucker headbutting me, biting my shoulders, and squirming his rock-hard baby body, in order to be done with me, to be returned to his mama, or even his granny, if we were over there.

Tucker and Mikaela's mama co-owned a consignment store with her own mother back then. When she went back work, both Tucker and Mikaela were in my care for many hours of the day, multiple days a week. I was not sad about that in any way; I was happy to be with them. But I did have some apprehensions, because at that time, Tucker, for the most part, really wanted nothing to do with me.

The first morning I was tending to the kids alone, I remembered the swing chair of Mikaela's infancy. It was in the dark, dank basement of our first house in North Minneapolis. I unearthed that contraption and set it up in the TV room.

If you remember what those things were like back in the 1970s and 1980s, you will know they weren't anywhere near as sophisticated, nor as ergonomically positive for a baby, as today's chairs are. Back then, you plopped your child in that sucker and turned the crank until you could crank no more. It then rocked your child at a speed that would be unacceptable to today's norms. But for Tucker, it was the equivalent of the two of us running toward each other in slow motion across a field of lilies.

The swing tamed the headbutting, shoulder-chomping-on-only-papa beast, and it was an immediate and wondrous relief to me. From that moment on, I had the secret to ease him whenever he needed easing.

Now, I didn't leave him in the room by himself, so that I could go watch mindless television for hours. I was always in the room with him. We connected. Tucker, Mikaela, and I figured it out, and the archaic cranking swing, straight out of *Green Acres*, was the machine that made it happen. It was beautiful.

In those toddler years, for both Tucker and Mikaela, we never needed any type of media or alternative entertainment option to fill their waking hours, because the two of them together was entertainment enough.

One of the countless blessings present each day in our first house together was the fact that their mama and I were both able to spend an enormous amount of time with the kids. Whether alone with them, or together with them, one of us was with them at nearly all times. If we weren't, they were with Granny and Buddy, right near our house. It was another place we all spent considerable time in.

Either their mama took one or both of the kids to her work, or I would haul the kids to my setups for gigs, to meetings, laundromats, grocery stores, gas stations . . . Whatever the need was, I didn't feel it was a burden to have them with me doing day-to-day things. We had fun together, and it always seemed to work with them.

I think because of those things, as well as the kids hanging out with all of the musicians I was working with at that time, mainly Mick Sterling and the Stud Brothers, the combination of early influences on them were vast and very positive. The kids were spoken to as friends. They were listened to. And when they were funny, as they often were, people gave them genuine laughs and affirmations of who they were.

In general, I think kids raised by at least one parent who is a musician have a rather positive and creative outlook on themselves and others. They've been in the trenches, and they've been spoken to as people. They've been listened to and not dismissed, or walked away from, as though they were a nuisance.

As Tucker and Mikaela grew, their hipness and cool quotient was off the chart to all who met them. Their base of friends was loyal, and both Mikaela and Tucker were champions of the underdogs and the mistreated. That started in elementary school and remained true all the way through their high school years.

Their love of great music, and their humor and sarcasm, were fed daily by my own warped sense of humor. It was further supplemented by *The Simpsons*. Their mama's love of literature seeped into both of them, and it molded who they were as young adults. And we were all better for it.

Both of the kids were live music roadies for me, helping at outdoor festivals and at the first big outdoor event I produced, an event called Heart & Soul. Heart & Soul benefited Camp Heartland, an organization that helped kids impacted by HIV and AIDS, by giving them a special, stigma-free summer camp to attend. Through these experiences, by the time Mikaela and Tucker entered the Twin Cities music scene, they had garnered the backstage knowledge to not be enamored, or intimidated, by musicians, agents, stage mangers, or others.

After high school, Mikaela became an intern for the legendary Sue McLean of Sue McLean & Associates. She loved Sue, and Sue loved her. Sue's office was above Bunker's Music Bar, the bar I played every Sunday for seventeen years. Bunker's was my musical home base. It was one of my proudest moments as a papa to drive Mikaela to her interview with Sue. I knew she'd nail it and she did.

Sue was the leading female promoter in the nation, and Mikaela was her trusted friend. Sue treated Mikaela as her peer. That is something I will never forget and will always be grateful for; Sue gave Mikaela such a remarkable benchmark in her life.

When Tucker graduated, we bought him a Fender bass guitar, a quite expensive one actually, but it was important he had a good one. I told him when we gave it to him that if he was good at this instrument, and just as important, if he was someone musicians wanted to hang out with, to be around to perform with, as a bass player he would never be out of a gig. Any genre of band always desires a strong bass player, and Tucker was certainly that. He grew into much more than that in the following years.

His first gig was with a band called The Jeff Wenberg Band. It was in Minneapolis at a joint named Brothers. Tucker had three days to learn the material because Jeff's bass player was no longer available, or got fired, or spontaneously combusted. I don't really remember. All I know is that Jeff needed a bass player. I told him about Tucker, and Tucker got the gig.

Three days later, Tucker was on stage with this band performing the first set. As I watched my son in his first professional show, performing songs he'd never played before in his life, I noticed he had no music charts. He had no music stand to hold the charts. He wasn't looking down on the ground at cheat sheets he may have made for the gig. I realized my son was a freak.

He'd memorized the entire first set. He never looked down. He knew all of the songs, the beginnings and the endings.

Here's a little peek inside the live band stuff for all of you nonmusicians:

In every band configuration from a trio on up, there are people on stage who can make a mistake and still make the song work. The keyboardist, the horn player, the drummer, and the guitarist can make mistakes, and, somehow, the song will get through. That luxury is not afforded to the bass player. The bass player needs to know everything at all times, or the song falls apart. That is why a great bass player is so treasured.

As Tucker finished his first set, I shared with him my wonder as to what he had accomplished. He had no idea that he should have charts, only that it was expected for him to know everything in each song. It was a tremendous indicator of the kind of musician he was and would become in future years.

Tucker's breadth of influences ranged from grunge to GWAR, from deep soul music to Americana. He liked rap and hip hop and many genres in between. That unique gumbo was the lifeblood of Tucker's trajectory as a guitarist and bass player. But if that wasn't enough, what emerged on top of that was his insanely unique and soulful voice.

With his high school buddies, Tucker formed a band called Brüder. From upstairs, we would hear Tucker's guttural screams as the band furiously grooved and rocked in his room in the lower level of the house. That's what I was used to. I thought that was his only voice. Thank God I was mistaken, because his other voices were a wonder.

In 2016, I produced an event for The 30-Days Foundation, a charity I founded and continue to direct. It was a live music event wherein multiple artists each performed one song. They got just one take, and that take would be recorded for a CD that would raise funds for The 30-Days Foundation. It was an event that featured some top Twin Cities talent from bands who wanted to contribute a song to help the charity. One of the artists was Tucker.

At the sound check for the event, I was sitting next to Ricky Peterson, one of the top keyboardists and Hammond organ players in the world. In 2019, Ricky was the organist for Fleetwood Mac in their nearly two-year world tour.

I did my sound check and sat out front to watch the others. Then, Tucker came up with his acoustic guitar and started singing. The room got silent.

His voice, his vibrato, the soft *S* sound that he had gotten from his mama; I called it "The Knutson Twang." His presence was all over the room, and my mouth was agape. I looked at Ricky while Tucker was singing, and I asked him, "Do I think Tucker is this good because he's my son, or is he really this good?!" We both laughed and agreed he was really that good.

I will never forget that sound coming out of him: a bit of me, a bit of Jonny Lang, a bit of James Curran, and a whole lot of his own impeccable choices. His lyrics were smart and unconventional, and as a lyricist myself, his thoughts fascinated me.

The choices he made on guitar, his tone, and his performance were completely unique. That evening, we felt that we were witnessing the birth of a major artist. It was staggeringly beautiful to see. As his papa, I realized he'd followed in not just my footsteps but also those of the musicians around us he had seen and clearly been influenced by.

Tucker's twenties were a grab bag of independent thought, actions, and strong work ethic. Music was his centerpiece, but he had varied interests, and conversations with him were intelligent, challenging, and filled with biting humor and sarcasm, an irresistible mix for his friends and the total strangers who were charmed by him.

He lived on his own or with friends. He was, for the most part, on the edge of not being able to pay bills. But pay bills he did; he did what needed to be done in order to be a single, independent musician, so he could feed the desire within him, to create, and to stimulate others to create.

In the early summer of 2016, Tucker was experiencing some bloating in his neck, face, and eyes. He was uncomfortable. He went to a couple of places, and they didn't really know what it was. When he told me about it, I wondered if he had been bitten by a tick or something similar to that to cause such a look. We really didn't know what it was, but he needed some relief because it was getting more difficult day by day. He went to one more place to find out what it was.

We found out.

I was getting set up to emcee the Lowertown Blues Fest in Mears Park in St. Paul when Tucker called. He said he'd found out what it was: lymphoma.

I'm not even able to describe what a father feels when that word is mentioned from his son. I could try to paint you a picture, but nothing I'd come up with would suffice. It was the worst phone call of my life. That's about the best I can do.

I drove back to the house, and Mama, Mikaela, and Tucker met me in the living room. We talked and planned. We then went and sat on the front steps and planned, and laughed, and planned some more, none of us saying how scared we were and how we really felt. It wasn't the time to do it. We had work to do.

Tucker received initial treatment at the Humphrey Cancer Center in Robbinsdale, Minnesota. He began his chemo sessions there, and the fine staff was, of course, in love with Tucker because of his cool demeanor and his sense of humor. Tucker was much younger than most of the patients at Humphrey, so that also contributed to his unique stature among the front staff, nurses, technicians, and his doctor, who got along famously with Tucker and with all of us.

The diagnosis for Hodgkin's lymphoma for a twenty-seven-year-old healthy male is very, very good. We were told 85-90 percent of the time the first chemo session can take care of it. We were told that if Tucker was going to have any cancer, this was a good one to have because of the statistics.

Tucker went into these sessions with a positive outlook and, for the most part, handled the chemo like a champ. He never complained, not once. As he completed his first round of chemo, we were all hoping to hear, and I think mostly expecting to hear, that Tucker was in the 90 percent, that he would get this taken care of and be able to begin his life again as a healthy person, one with cancer, but healthy.

That didn't happen.

We were told that the chemo did not work, and his next sessions would have to be at the Masonic Cancer Center at the University of Minnesota.

The University of Minnesota stint of Tucker's treatments was more intense. It included multiple hospital stays because of ailments caused by the intensive treatment. He would be in the hospital for five to ten days, just to get back to a level that was stable enough to continue the scheduled treatment plans.

For multiple hours each day and evening, all of us, but especially Mikaela, would be at the hospital visiting Tucker. Mikaela was always Tucker's closest confidant and friend, just as he was to her. I have never seen siblings as close and in sync as the two of them were. They were that way as little children, and they still were as grown adults.

Tucker's mama and I did what we could to comfort Tucker, while Mikaela basically laid down her social life and adapted her entire world to be able to be there for her brother as often, and as long, as she could be. Her dedication to Tucker was not a surprise to any of us.

One afternoon when Tucker was still in the early stages of treatment at the Masonic Center, we had the opportunity to have lunch after his treatment. I loved our conversations because he was just so damned interesting and funny, and he made me raise my game, in my never-ending effort to try and make him laugh, just to be in his league. Everybody knew, if you made Tucker laugh, you had to have said something pretty funny.

In our conversation that day, while I was waiting for his treatment to complete, I shared an observation I'd had. I said to him that most musicians of any worth, those who are strong at their instrument and their songwriting, always wish they had more time to do two things: they wish they could spend more time practicing their instrument, and they wish they could spend more time songwriting. Most musicians never achieve that goal because they're always so busy trying to earn a living.

I told Tucker that in some god-awful way, he had been afforded this opportunity that musicians always want but never get. I told him that if he felt up to it, and was not so fatigued as to prohibit him, this cancer, this time away from work and the responsibilities of bills, could provide him his opportunity to write his masterpiece. Friends, coworkers, and peers of mine, some of whom had known Tucker since he was a baby, had made generous contributions to help him through the treatment period.

So, that is exactly what he did.

If you search for Tucker's band, Dirt Train, and his solo work on YouTube, you will notice that the vast majority, if not all of the videos, are of Tucker at various stages of chemo. Hair, no hair, a little bit of hair, thin, not as thin, etc. Songwriting, arranging, playing live at The Terminal Bar in Minneapolis (to a basically empty room) one night a week, all so Dirt Train could work on their material and become a stronger band.

His dedication to the band and to The Terminal Bar was so strong that one night Tucker left the hospital after a particularly hellish day of chemo and, twenty minutes later, entered the barroom to play a gig to the delight and cheers of his bandmates. This was the kind of work ethic and bravery Tucker showed to everyone he met. It was a marvel to witness. I was so proud of what he accomplished, as all of us were.

In the summer of 2018, Tucker and his mama went to Arizona to try some different routes of therapy. We were looking for an alternative to stem cell treatments, which, while they say are effective at times, are quite brutal and require long hospital stays with less guarantee of success than what Tucker had originally hoped for back at the Humphrey Cancer Center.

That quest did not last long, because, at that time, Tucker's health was on an upswing, and, as he told me, he did not want to be around a bunch of sick people who were older than him. I could understand his frustration. Despite the frustration his mama felt, for she wanted to give it more of a try, Tucker came back home to continue his treatments in the Twin Cities and to get back with his band to write and perform new music.

In early 2019, things for Tucker started getting more severe. By this time, he was in his fourth and fifth rounds of some variation of chemo, and he had multiple hospital stays. In the succession of a few weeks, he had pneumonia and shingles. Those two setbacks began the final downward path for Tucker, as he spent more and more time in one of the floors at the University of Minnesota hospital.

The schedule, beginning around February of that year, was mainly Mikaela being there all the time, Mama being there a few hours during the day and early evening, and me staying overnight as many nights as possible and then going to my day job around 5:00 a.m. each morning.

Those early days of February were extremely difficult for Tucker. His breathing was horribly labored, and he was exhausted. Seeing your child struggle with each breath is beyond difficult to witness.

The constant visits of hospital staff and doctors interrupted any type of real sleep Tucker could attain, and with his labored breathing, it was frustratingly evident that Tucker could get no rest. Without rest, how could he possibly get himself in a position to start a new treatment, or to improve at all?

During this time, I was reminded of a gut feeling I'd had months prior at the Masonic Cancer Center, when we were told by Tucker's second doctor that the second round of chemo still did not work.

We were all stunned as we listened to his doctor tell us that the past few weeks of treatments had not accomplished what we'd all wanted. And though the doctor's face was blocked by her mask, my gut was screaming at me that her explanation to us was filled with words she couldn't say. Words like, "I hate to tell you this, but I've regrettably seen this before. And I can't tell you that, because there are other options to explore first." Or, "I hate my job right now so very much, and I'm so sorry for all of you." That doctor had seen this film before, and she just didn't want to share with us what I think she knew at that meeting.

I couldn't shake that feeling that day. I hated that day.

I hated what was happening to Tucker.

I hated that his mama had to see her boy go through this.

I hated the thousand-pound anvil of pain, fright, and responsibility that Mikaela felt, watching her brother go through this.

I hated that Tucker felt so bad for us, watching him go through that.

I hated how scared Tucker must have been, and how he hid it to protect all of us. He was so damned brave through all of it. But we all loved Tucker, and we kept going and remained hopeful, despite what we were fearing inside. As did he.

On March 1st, I received a call from Mikaela prior to a show I was doing in Minneapolis. She said I needed to come right away to the ICU, because they were saying there was a chance Tucker would not survive the night. I rushed to the hospital and saw Mama and Mikaela in the room, and together, we started the nearly eleven-day encampment in the University of Minnesota ICU, to be there for Tucker in his final days.

When you're in a hospital, time and the outside world seem not so present. Because what is within your presence is so all-encompassing, nothing seems to really matter outside of that. Tucker, in the ICU, was certainly the most extreme version of that we had ever felt. The three of us in the ICU together transformed and grew to include visitors, family, and friends, converging on the room and in all parts of the ICU level.

Mikaela and Tucker's friends started to converge on the ICU in the early days. Their mutual best friends stayed for the duration of those eleven days, sleeping on the waiting room floor or in chairs each night, just to be there for both of them. Family members were coming and visiting Tucker and trying to lend support to all three of us as well. This mix of friends and family created the support system that the three of us needed during the most horrific period of our lives.

In the late afternoon of the first Saturday of Tucker's time in the ICU, we had the talk. It is the worst talk you can have as a parent, or be part of as a sibling. It is the worst talk a family can have.

I listened intently during the worst talk we'd ever have, because everything was the most important thing I had ever heard. At the same time, I was in such a terrifying and sad fog, that I wouldn't be able to recite anything to you today if asked what was said. I know only the basic structure: our approval of what was to happen if matters got to that point. It was as if everything was being spoken to us in the saddest and most disgusting language ever uttered.

As we finished, we were notified that the members of Dirt Train, the band Tucker led, were downstairs and could come up at any time. We invited them up immediately. We all hugged the guys, let them in to visit Tucker, and closed the glass door behind us as we left them alone with Tucker in his room. In a couple minutes after we left the room, as a few of us were talking outside Tucker's door, I glanced in and saw a miracle.

Where just ten minutes ago Tucker had been lying back in his bed with his mask on feeling terrible, he was now sitting up, gesturing to all of his band members. And all of them were laughing their asses off. It was, I think, the most miraculous vision I've ever seen. Everything was different from just minutes prior. It was an opening; an awakening is perhaps a better description. It was God. It had to be. Who else could have created such finely orchestrated perfection for our boy at that moment?

I got on the phone with his band leader and dear friend, Ken Valdez, and told him to come to the ICU immediately because Tucker was in a better place to talk. Then I called his boss and friend, Caleb Garn, and others and told them to come, too. Thus began a period of precious hours when Tucker was alert enough, and awake enough, to be a closer version of the Tucker we all loved and knew.

God gave us that time with Tucker, I am convinced of that. It was a glorious time for all of us, as short-lived as it turned out to be.

As the days passed, there were over fifty friends and family members who descended upon the ICU to be there for Tucker. For the three of us, it was a constant succession of highs and lows, of new information to gather and share with Tucker.

There was a lot of pacing and hugs and explanations to people wanting updates on Tucker. There was a lot of consoling people who were worried about us and how we were doing. But at times, even during the constant struggle Tucker went through, he still showed glimpses of himself, as he conjured up something clever and wickedly funny, to knock us down laughing.

The attending physician on the weekdays was different from the weekend attending. We had never seen the doctor who showed up on the second Saturday Tucker was in the ICU. Some of the nurses were the same. Our main nurse was still present, thankfully, because she was incredible. And another new one was also with us in the room, and she was equally spectacular at taking care of Tucker, and of us.

The attending who had never met Tucker spoke to him in front of a room full of staff and immediate family. He asked Tucker the same questions Tucker had been answering for weeks with different doctors, on different floors, or in the ICU. As he asked his questions, I noticed Tucker's eyes. I could tell something was going on in his head, but I had no idea what.

One thing everyone knew about Tucker was that his comedic timing was impeccable. Despite how awful Tucker was feeling (and by that time, it was hell for him) that instinct of his was still intact.

The attending finished his examination and wished Tucker the best, saying he'd see him again later on. He offered all the pleasantries that can possibly be stated in that kind of medical situation, then he turned around, opened the door, and left. The instant the door shut, Tucker took off his breathing mask and, smirking, said, "I thought that (descriptive and perfectly delivered expletive only Tucker could have said so artfully) would never leave!"

There was a silence and stillness in the room for a brief moment until the whole room erupted with laughter. It was a welcome reminder that this brilliant young man, dealing with something so massive, with such bravery that it boggles the mind, still felt it important within his soul to provide comfort and humor to all of us who were so sad for him.

That was our boy. That was Tucker all over the place.

There came a time shortly after that day when he had a particularly restless night, and it was evident that our time with Tucker was drawing near to an end. The unfortunate muscle that, as a parent, you dread to flex, the muscle that gets activated when you have to manage everything that will follow with family, with friends, with arrangements and services, and where and how it will all take place . . . that muscle kicked in. We were there.

Because Tucker was a Minneapolis boy, and because so many people knew Tucker and Mikaela, from their professional time in the music business, from my long history of performing in the Twin Cities, and from Mikaela's time working for Sue McLean & Associates, I knew we could not do the service at a suburban church that would only hold a couple hundred people. There could easily be a thousand people at the service to honor Tucker. So, I called the Basilica of St. Mary in Minneapolis. It made sense and seemed fitting that a life such as Tucker's would be honored in such a grand building.

Thankfully, despite us not being members at the Basilica, they listened to my story of Tucker and what we needed in order to honor him, and they allowed us time in the historic Basilica to have a service for Tucker. That was a heavy burden, to arrange something that no one ever wants to arrange for their child.

More doctors came throughout that period of final hours. They gave us the talk and the look. The attending nurses and physicians had all connected strongly with Tucker, and with our family, during this time. I understand it is their job to show compassion at times like this, and they are very good at it. But they are not actors. Even Brando and Streep aren't *that* good of actors. That staff was not acting. Those were real tears, real laughs, and real tenderness, shown to all of us, and to Tucker, in his final days.

For one final time, Dirt Train visited Tucker, just them. As I walked down the hall to Tucker's room, they were all walking toward me with such pain in their faces. They knew what followed, and it broke their hearts. It broke my heart seeing them crying, while at the same time, I was so grateful, even then, that they'd had a chance to be alone with their friend and leader in their own way, without others around. The final band meeting.

It was decided that at a certain time of the day, Tucker was going to be put on an extremely high dose of medication to comfort him as much as possible. Nearly seventy-five people gathered in the ICU waiting rooms and hallways. They were pacing and talking nervously, as various family members and friends said their goodbyes, without physical acknowledgment from Tucker that he comprehended them. I like to think he did.

Finally, it was just the four of us alone in the room again. The nurse came and administered the medication to provide comfort. The breathing apparatus kept its steady rhythm. The three of us spoke softly, staring at Tucker and at each other. We were suspended in that reserve God gives everyone during times like this, to do what needs to be done in the moment, despite the overwhelming sadness all around us. In the first five minutes of this process, it was complete. Our boy in front of us was no longer with us. He was blessedly out of pain, and the dreaded pivot happened: the one that must always take place within families when someone they love passes.

As soon as Tucker passed, the depth of love for him in the Twin Cities music community shone so brilliantly, and dominated social media for such a long time, that it graced and honored all of us. It was just beautiful.

The impact Tucker made was unmistakable, and as the days followed, we all found out how deep his roots were, how many people he influenced and inspired in his far-too-short time with us. Continued blessings such as these, despite the buckling sadness we were feeling, were a counterbalance, helping us get through this unspeakable time.

Things get done how and when they are supposed to during times like these. There are no events of this size that get organized as quickly and come together as efficiently as the arrangements for a funeral service. Thankfully, despite some tiny hiccups, the service for Tucker went very smoothly.

With help from organizations like MusicCares, and from our dear friend Miki Mulvehill, who owns Heart & Soul Artist Management, the service and all the expenses were thankfully covered.

As I drove with my sister Jessica to the Basilica the morning of the service, I couldn't fathom that we were driving to my son's funeral. My son's funeral. But we had a job to do, a face to put on, a service to complete, and an honoring of his life to get through, in a way only the three remaining members of this remarkable family could do. And we did it. My God, did we do it.

The service for Tucker was filled with such a blessed combination of simple, direct love and appropriate religious pageantry that it was not just visually palatable, but spiritually too; even for those uncomfortable in settings such as the Basilica, it was undeniably and unquestionably loving.

The eulogies presented by Mama, Mikaela, and me were preceded by a once-in-a-lifetime version of "Amazing Grace" sung by Rachel Kurtz and lovingly performed by Tucker's bandmate "Lightnin'" Joe Peterson. To this day, their rendition is mentioned to me as being one of the greatest versions of that song people have ever heard. And it was; it was stunning.

And then, the family that saw Tucker through the thousands of ridiculously cute things he'd done as a baby, a toddler, a young child, and a teenager, did what needed to be done.

Our son, Mikaela's brother, needed to have words said about him, in the grandeur of the Basilica, in our own deeply personal way.

All of Tucker and Mikaela's friends from their school years have known us so long that they call us Mama and Papa. That's what Tucker and Mikaela called us, so that's how their friends knew us. That was fine with us. It was time for Mama and Papa and their daughter to tell the stories of Tucker in ways only we knew. We spoke of the experiences that molded Tucker and Mikaela into the people their dear, lifelong friends, who were surrounding us with love in the Basilica that day, knew them to be.

Mikaela spoke first. She is the one person who knew Tucker better than anyone. She was our champion and leader through all of the hardships and pain we were feeling. She spoke with such love and strength; it was momentous.

Mama then told multiple stories from Tucker's youth. Her words were those that can only come from a mother who loves her boy as much as Mama loved Tucker. She spoke of Tucker's beauty as a soul on this earth. The mama was strong, and loving, and her strength during this unspeakable time was noticed by everyone. She was the mama that all their friends knew and loved. Tucker and Mikaela's mama was brilliant.

As I walked up to honor Tucker, I stood silently, and I looked out at the nearly one thousand people gathered inside the Basilica. I let the magnitude of the moment wash over me. The honoring of our boy was breathtaking to me. I then began.

I shared old stories of Tucker as a child, stories that were, of course, as adorable as he was. They got big laughs. I spoke of Tucker's spirit, humor, and intelligence, of how loved he was by his family, and how I couldn't have dreamt of a better son. I didn't need a script; I knew what I wanted to say. I lived it.

But while I was speaking, I felt it was necessary to state quite clearly how important this passing was for all of his friends. It was their first big one. The first big loss in their lives. I wanted to acknowledge this to all his peers and friends who were in attendance. They needed a papa at that moment, and I couldn't have been prouder to be in that role.

Later, when the service was over and we were all gathered in the lower level, I wanted everyone to know that while we appreciated their kind words to us, and their realizations of what we as a family were going through, and how much harder it must have been, even, to what they were feeling, it was unnecessary to equate their level of pain to ours. There was no way they could feel what we felt, and there was no way we could feel what they felt as his friends. One pain doesn't take a back seat to another pain; they are simply just two different pains.

The common thread between all of us was that what had just happened to Tucker was just awful, and we hated it and we will always hate it. We missed Tucker in that church that day. We still do. We always will.

This is a terrible club to belong to. I don't recommend it; it's awful. But as with every sad thing, some beauty can emerge.

It did emerge through all of this. The love from Tucker's care-givers over the course of those two years will never be forgotten. They were such fine people.

The respect shown from all of Tucker's friends, how they never posted one thing about his cancer on social media the entire time he had it, was as honoring as they could be to their friend; they respected Tucker's wishes, and it was beautiful. We live in a society where having a hangnail gets posted to Facebook. That made the silence surrounding Tucker's cancer even more astounding and honorable.

The otherworldly strength of Mikaela, caring for every need of the brother she loved so much, despite her unique, gut-level, daily pain, defined my daughter in myriad ways. She will draw upon that strength for the rest of her life, and her friends will be blessed because of it. She carries Tucker with her every day.

The moment Dirt Train came to cheer Tucker up, and when they walked from his room one last time, will be etched in my soul forever. It will never leave me. The depth of that kind of brotherly love and musical bond is sadly beautiful, and I'll cherish it. It goes on and on, honestly.

Every day is never the same when you've lost a child. I find myself going through a day or evening being just fine, and then whether I'm awake or it's in my dreams, I either get kicked in the gut, or my emotions overwhelm me. On March 15th of 2020, mass gatherings, including funerals for loved ones, were shut down because of COVID-19. Every day since then, I've been incredibly grateful we did not experience Tucker's passing in 2020.

The scenario of losing our boy without having experienced the extraordinary outpouring of love in the ICU, and the grandeur and loveliness of his service at the Basilica, is unthinkable and unimaginable to me. It would have cheated all of those who loved our boy so much their opportunity to say what they needed to say, and to look at him one more time to laugh or cry.

For twenty-nine years, Tucker graced our lives. Why it was so short is not for us to know. We can only speculate and wish it was not so.

His tenacity and intelligence inspire me daily. To attempt anything and everything I think I'm capable of, even if I fail, is worth trying.

Tucker inspired those who knew and loved him to create their own masterpieces.

Our boy was a good boy.

I'm having trouble focusing at the
"Hard to Listen To" Festival today.

The Community
Called Community

I'm reminded again of the unlimited potential of community. How community binds us, molds us, and gives us, yes, a sense of *community*.

I wish I would have known about community when I was younger. That way, I would never have had to be alone when I went through such exhilarating childhood experiences as shame, fear, guilt, awkwardness with girls, awkwardness with my raging hormones, acne, peer pressure, and a dozen other developmental issues.

If I had accessed the community that was nearby, all of these issues would have disappeared, because the community would not have expected me to learn anything from defeats and successes. The community doesn't believe in wins and losses. The community has only fairness, and avoids feelings being hurt.

As a matter of fact, in the community hall, inside the township of Communityville, that is the written charter for the Community Chamber of Commerce. It's not inspiring, nor discouraging; it just makes me feel a sense of community when I see it. And that is nice. Don't you think?

In my professional life as a musician, I am part of a community.

A community of musicians, singers, writers, critics, guitar technicians, promoters, booking agents, and more. We are a community. While we certainly do things for others in our community, to assist another community member at a time of need or peril, we don't adhere quite so strongly to the idea of "fairness" within the community. Not when it comes to our own individual success in the community of the music business . . .

There are common bonds in the community I belong to: bad gigs, good gigs, not getting paid for a gig, bad audiences, great audiences . . . No matter what level you are at as a musician, these things happen to you. But what of one of the most important tenets of the community? The idea that in a true community, being fair to yourself *and* to others is of the utmost importance, and actually supersedes nearly everything else? Because in the end, it's better to be fair than not to be fair.

But think about the teenage version of the blues phenom Jonny Lang. He tore it up for years, in this town and around the country, and he sold more CDs than any other completely fantastic Twin Cities icon at that time. Was that fair? If we were a true community, it would not be fair to nearly every other veteran singer-songwriter or band at that time, because the veterans had been in the community working hard for far longer than Jonny. So why him and not any of them?

If the music business were completely fair, every veteran musician in this town should have received the same level of success as Jonny, Shannon Curfman, Brother Ali, Dessa, Prince, or even Dylan, for that matter. They have certainly done it as long as the others, so they, too, should reap the reward of their experience, shouldn't they?

If it were fair, wouldn't it stand to reason that Jonny should have taken all his money that came from touring and recording, and spread it around to the others in his community? Wasn't Jonny part of the community we were all a part of, after all?

If we're part of a community, and a community doesn't wish ill will against others in the same community, why, in those days, were so many musicians in this town so envious and jealous of Jonny's success?

Should someone within a community not be able to exceed the perceived limitations of that community?

Was Jonny being unfair to his community because he didn't share his financial success with all of us? Of course he wasn't.

Was it his fault he possessed an intoxicating combination of youth, talent, and passion, and that these attributes attracted a Twin Cities audience larger than that of any other artist I'd ever seen in clubland? Yes, I believe it was Jonny Lang's fault for being exceptional. It's not very fair that he was perceived as more exceptional than the others, myself included, but he simply was, and he deserved all of the success he had and still has.

The sad truth is, it's not very community-considerate to be exceptional. It makes people feel bad, and in turn, it makes the community feel bad.

The community I belong to believes in helping each other as community members. But at the same time, musicians have to do some very noncommunity-minded things if they want to achieve a level of success above that of their local communities and become national recording artists. That level of success requires a musician to do things that are perceived as exceptional in order to rise above their community.

In the end, while the music community is a vocal champion for fairness in other professions, the only reason any success happens in the music business is because of unfairness: the unfairness of exceptionalism, charisma, timing, and connections with an audience, with performance, with songs. Those things have no set rule.

Those are gut reactions that happen when a new listener sees a performer, or hears a song, and becomes a die-hard fan. Those who have achieved national and international success in this business worked damned hard for that gut reaction, and they deserve all of the success they are having, despite it perhaps not feeling fair to others who have been doing it as long as they have. It's just life, and sometimes, life ain't fair.

Thank God this business is not based on fairness, or the entire industry would be a watered-down, boring waste of time.

If you have a music hero who inspires you, that hero is a hero to you because they shined in your eyes. They stood tall over the rest.

It wasn't fair they shined brighter than others who are, perhaps, as talented. But for some mysterious reason, their shine caught your eye, and it transformed your life. That hero rose above whatever community may have molded him or her at one time, and more often than not, that same community will turn their back on the one who rises above them. I've seen it happen many times, and it will happen many more times.

This is a community-based world we live in. In multiple ways, it's a good thing to be in a community. But be careful about counting too much on a sense of community. For if you do, you limit the growth of your successes, and the learning potential of your losses.

The community can fortress you from many things, but there are things you need to learn and experience on your own in order for you to become the person you know, or don't know, you can be. If you don't occasionally fail when you put it all on the line, how do you learn anything? If you win all the time, how can you enjoy it? You won't, if it's commonplace.

It's like that old episode of *The Twilight Zone* where the gambler thinks he's in heaven because he keeps winning all the time; then he starts getting bored with it. He starts complaining about heaven, and they tell him, who said you were in heaven?

I'm weary of the word community. It's overused. Its meaning is weakened, and because of that, it doesn't accomplish what it used to. Because it seems to me a community used to be a group of people striving to, one day, rise above their community, to strengthen the community they emerged from. Now, it seems like what we want is for our community to wrap us up in a warm blanket, so that we stand a lesser chance of being treated unfairly, or of our feelings being hurt by the occasional, inevitable failures.

We've got one shot at this life. I don't want to spend my entire time in a blanket. Do you?

I want to honor those in my community who have achieved higher levels of success than me. I don't want to bring them down because I'm envious of them. What am I, twelve years old? I'm a nearly sixty-year-old man who understands that success does not come easily. So when it comes at all to others in this business, or in any business for that matter, I say, "Bravo!"

I'm not saying I'm against the concept of community, or against feeling a sense of community. I'm just saying we should be careful how much we depend on our community. It may not be serving us as well as we think.

Sometimes you have to break from your community, so that you can create a community that expects more than the one that molded you.

I know what you're thinking, and I concur. Saturn is not a real planet. It's more of a galactic hamlet.

Escape from
the Card Tables

I wish I could tell you that when I'm singing on stage I am completely focused on what I am doing. In many ways, I am focused on the song, the lyric, and how my performance is being viewed by the public.

But there is a piece of my brain that always seems to wander, and I find myself delving into moments from my past and present, or things I'm hoping will or won't happen in the future.

I don't know if I'm alone with this malady, but nevertheless, I live with it.

The other night when I was singing, I started thinking about how important card tables were in my life.

Yes, card tables.

Specifically, I thought about what the card table meant to my early development from a small boy to a young teenager and, finally, to adulthood.

As flimsy and beaten down as the majority of those card tables were, the power of those four rickety legs, and of the flat surface, which always seemed to slope in the middle, was palpable.

The card table defines childhood.

You would think something of such importance in a household would be placed in a well-traveled, viewable area, on display when you enter your home, like in your kitchen or living room. But for some mysterious reason, the card table is always found in the hall closet, behind the winter coats, leaning against thirty-seven photo albums, atop the old mousetrap that your parents set four years ago, which has yet to yield a result.

The first sign of your upcoming, yet light-years-away, adulthood status is when you are asked to retrieve the card table from its dark, spiderweb-filled lair.

Your little arms and legs have to contort in order for you to retrieve it, but retrieve it you will, dammit, because company is coming. Company is coming!

The card table is normally placed no more than ten feet from the grown-ups' table. It is placed there for many reasons.

The main reasons are purely based on reach for the adults. Although it's true the adults want you to eat the food they prepared, on this particular evening, once they sit down to eat, they really don't want to get up very often in order to accommodate your food needs.

The ten-foot distance also works so the adults can be within earshot of anything that they should be hearing, but still far enough away to be able to ignore all the silly, indecipherable things that are going to be said at the card table.

The card table is also an introduction to how to handle yourself when you are forced to dine with complete strangers. Think of it as a wedding reception for toddlers through teenagers. Most of the time at family functions, you are stuck at a table with cousins you have nothing in common with, and whom you have only seen once or twice in your life.

If you're a boy, the card table forces you to be friends with the only other boy there who is your age, even if you've never met that boy and think he's weird, boring, or just annoying. The same goes for girls.

The card table is a miniature version of the United Nations: strangers sitting down, speaking different languages, forced to get along. It rarely works the way it should in either scenario.

The card table educates you in the fact that being a kid doesn't mean you get everything you want. Because despite the fact that you really have nothing in common with the grown-ups at the big table, the fact that you can't sit there tells you that you are not yet at their same level.

As you sit on the rusty folding chair with your elbows on the raised, rounded edges of the card table, you bide your time, dreaming of the day when you will be big and intelligent enough to sit at the big table.

The card table also teaches you about space economics.

The big table has room for the roast, mashed potatoes, corn, beans, salt, pepper, coffee, beverages, and centerpieces, not to mention the main plate, salad plate, silverware, and serving bowls. The card table has room for paper plates and a few little plates with limited samples of the bounty that rests at the big table.

The lack of food at the card table gives you a fighting chance to clean your plate quicker, so you can escape the awkwardly forced confinement that is the card table. In a perfect world, the clean plate / early escape plan would always work. But it never does. Why?

Because no one leaves the card table alive until the adults are good-and-ready for you to leave.

Dinner is now done. You are sitting at the card table with empty plates, either having nothing to say, or being forced to listen to some relative you barely know, who won't shut up about something that means nothing to you. Or perhaps you're sitting at the card table with a really cute girl, who, unfortunately, turns out to be your hot-looking cousin. During this interminable awkwardness, you witness laughter and intelligent conversation at the big table, and it seems it will never end. It's not that you begrudge your parents a good time, but how long are they going to laugh and tell the same stories over and over? Like a bobcat stuck in a steel trap, you want out, and you want out now.

The older you get, the more responsibility you have for the card table. You retrieve it. You put the tablecloth on it. You set up the silverware and arrange the food on it. Your desire to one day eat at the big table is still there, but as you get older, your card table privileges advance.

You're not beholden to the same rules that the much younger kids at the table must obey. There is a certain age you hit when you're no longer expected to entertain the smaller ones, and your time of freedom from the card table arrives sooner than it used to.

The card table teaches you to never expect anything, no matter how much sense it makes to you. I've heard tales of seventeen-year-olds having to endure the card table, while others of the same age found themselves at the big table. It would seem age, and actual physical size, would dictate your time at the card table, but that's not always the case.

The moment you aren't expected to sit at the card table is a mysterious and magical transformation that no one really understands.

There are some tried-and-true reasons that you won't be expected to sit at the card table anymore. If your shoe size grows past an eleven, that sets you free.

If you have facial hair, or you got your girlfriend pregnant, that sets you free in one way (and at the same time, gives you a whole hell of a lot more to be concerned about than your never-ending stint at the card table). If you got your girlfriend pregnant, purchasing your own card table is certainly in your future.

My feeling is, the best way to free yourself from the card table is to know when to speak, and when to shut up. The card table gives you the chance to understand the flow of language and replicate the nuances of the adults nearby.

You have to understand the things they are talking about and either learn about those topics or find a way to fake it well enough; that way, when you are around adults, they think you're interested in what they are saying.

Just like a performer, you have to know your audience. Knowing what's funny, and what's not funny, is also good. You have to understand that everything in your head, despite how interesting it is to you, is probably not that interesting to adults.

In most cases, the quickest way to leave behind the card table for good is knowing what to say and when to say it. Now that I always sit at the big table, I have fond memories of the card table. The card table is constant and fleeting at the same time. It's something we all have to endure.

It's comforting to know that the tradition of awkwardness will continue, because it's from that awkwardness that we learn.

Criticism drew criticism yesterday as critical critiques were criticized rather critically, during The Critical Festival in Criticismville this past weekend.

The World According to Musicians' Pieholes

Watching paint dry.

Watching soccer or golf alone.

Reading the phone book from a town you don't live in.

These are boring things to do. But none of these boring activities compares to the level of boredom nonmusicians feel when they hear musicians complaining about how hard it is to be a musician.

It's certainly true that being a musician can be difficult and disheartening. The career can cause pain and heartache.

But rest assured, when a musician regales a nonmusician with a tale of woe, while the nonmusician may react sympathetically, beneath that reaction there is a sense that the musician has no reason to complain about anything.

You are a musician who gets paid to play music, after all. How bad can it really be?

There are no other jobs that receive applause as often, or as rapidly, as a musician does. The only career that would come close would be a tennis player who always aces, who consistently wipes the floor with his opponent.

Even if the applause is "a smattering," it is more than non-musicians receive for doing the jobs they are paid for.

So why would a person who receives applause complain about the job that garners this applause, especially to a person who never receives applause at all? Or to describe it à la *Seinfeld*, "Who leaves a country packed with ponies to come to a non-pony country?" Why would a musician who has multiple ponies complain to a person who is ponyless?

The truth is, the vast majority of people have little to no interest in how hard it is for a musician to cut it in LA or Nashville. They just think it's damned cool that you are in LA or Nashville.

They have little to no interest in how much money musicians make in clubland. "If you don't like how much money you make as a musician," they think, "get a different job that pays you more." They don't care about the quality of the room a musician plays in, or whether it's seen as cool, sucky, fantastic, or horrific.

Because all they see is that you are a musician. You get to play music for people, no matter what the room is like. It's something they could never imagine doing. They may not have the musical ability to do it.

The truth is, grumbling about how hard it is to be a musician should be kept within the family of musicians. Grumble to ourselves, musicians. It's our best shot at a sympathetic audience.

Because despite the fact that others around you portray sympathy, they are likely just trying to be nice by listening. Deep down, they don't really have a lot of sympathy for our stories.

A few years ago, I was listening to a Twin Cities classic rock station called KQRS, and I heard an Aerosmith song. I can't remember the title of it. It has words and chords. You know, that one song they do. I like the song a lot, though. I like Aerosmith a lot.

They wrote incredible songs. I love how they sound. I love Joe Perry and Steven Tyler. I even like the one or two guys who make Steven and Joe look prettier. It's the tried-and-true Rod Stewart method, to make the leader the best-looking guy in the band. Aerosmith are musical icons. Their songs will be played for decades on radio stations all around the world, because their songs are that good.

The announcer was talking about Joe Perry's latest book and what he'd written about his time in Aerosmith. I have also seen bios and news reports about the band. They frequently discuss how much stress there was in the band, and how much the bandmates didn't like each other. As a musician, you know what I think when I hear that? Stop spoiling my love of your band!

I don't want to know how hard it is to be in Aerosmith. You're AEROSMITH!!! I love your songs. They are spectacular songs, and you are spectacular live performers. You are superstars.

You contributed to the musical landscape with songs that are known around the world. You are wealthy beyond your wildest dreams. You have done the one thing that you wanted to do, and you've done it your entire adult life. Why are you complaining while millions of musicians who play in clubs, VFWs, and wedding bands are being asked to turn their volume down so that one person at the bar can hear himself speak as he watches the season-opening rugby match between Zimbabwe and Scotland?

While it's intriguing to know what happens behind the scenes of any famous band, in the end, do we really want to know?

If I know a band's members hate each other, it affects how I hear their music. Yes, tension between band members can create better music. That has happened. But when does legitimate tension turn into illegitimate whining? As a fan, do you really want to hear that? I don't think I really do, even as a musician.

I want to be naive and idealistic. I want to believe the creators of these incredible works really dig being in the position to make life-altering music, the kind that affects us all once we hear it.

Complaining will always be part of any job. I just wonder if it's better for the fan, and for the musician, to keep the complaining within the four walls of musicianhood. Because the rest of the people—they just want to hear some rock 'n' roll!

It's not polite to point. It's also not polite to throw a pie at a hummingbird.

The Mancini Principle

In my mid-to-late twenties, I was a waiter at a restaurant that is no longer around. It was called The American Café. It was connected to a place called CocoLezzone, which was owned by two brothers, Rick and David Webb. Connected to these restaurants was a nightclub called Rupert's, which was incredibly hot in the 1980s and 1990s. This place was the centerpiece of an array of music, culture, and debauchery. People tell tall tales about what they participated in at Rupert's.

My job as a waiter at The American Café saved my butt for multiple reasons. I was a new family man and was not yet working as a musician. Thankfully, that changed fast. Within less than a year, Mick Sterling and the Stud Brothers started getting known in the Twin Cities, and I stopped being a waiter. The band was just playing too much. But I loved that job. I loved the people I was working with, and just like the clubgoers at Rupert's, I have stories to tell about my time as a waiter.

There was a round table that could seat up to eight people. It was right next to the kitchen door we would go in and out of when serving the customers. I used to work the breakfast and lunch shifts, and this table would be inhabited by the same six-to-eight businessmen at least four-to-five times per week. They would conduct business and hurl BS at each other for hours.

This was their table. When they were there, they were the kings of the restaurant. They all had very specific orders, and each time they arrived, all of us were prepped prior to going to their table. These gentlemen were important. They needed to be tended to perfectly. If, for some reason, service was not up to their standards, or if the food they were eating was subpar, the entire table's bill was comped.

It seemed extreme to me at the time for management to go this far to satisfy these guys. But the bigger picture was far more important than any one tab.

These guys weren't going anywhere. This was their home away from home. This was their place. Management knew they would come in twenty times a month and spend money every time. If one or two of the experiences needed to be comped for them to pay eighteen or nineteen other times each month, the loss was well worth it.

Because of our long-standing back-and-forth with these guys, management and staff also became fodder for their humor and sarcasm. We became like family to these guys, and they treated us well the vast majority of the times they visited us.

My mother, Neva Wickstrom, was one of the great servers and restaurant managers in the Twin Cities. From her, I learned the flow of a restaurant and what made it tick. The Webb brothers taught me how important the intangible things are. Those human things that can't be put on an expense sheet, such as decisions about how to treat customers, actually dictated the success of their business. What they did was not rocket science, but it was clear to me then, and is still clear decades later, that very few restaurants and bars know their simple secret of success. Most eventually fail.

In my performance career, I have been around the great club owners in the Twin Cities. I was always grateful to be in their employ.

James and Jackie Klein, who ran Bunker's Music Bar in the Warehouse District of Minneapolis, were amazing club owners. They were also the first to provide me with any type of real attention in the Twin Cities music scene. Bunker's became the home base for Mick Sterling and the Stud Brothers. Steve McLellan, who ran First Avenue and 7th St. Entry, was also one of the greats. Likewise, Billy Larson and Karen Palm, when they were together, did a great job with the Minnesota Music Cafe in St. Paul. For decades, Lowell Pickett has run the legendary Dakota in downtown Minneapolis. It is always a thrill to perform there.

These places all adhere to the same philosophy followed by the Webb brothers. They focus on their base and do everything they can to keep their clientele coming back. The Webb brothers' success in those early days was evidence this approach worked.

Recently, as an independent contractor, I worked as the booking agent for Mancini's Char House in St. Paul. There, I had the pleasure of getting to know Pat Mancini, son of the original owner, Nick Mancini. Around the same time, I also began working with a wonderful new nightclub called Crooners, which is in Fridley, Minnesota, just north of Minneapolis. The longstanding success of Mancini's and the relatively new, significant rise of Crooners have been interesting to witness.

Mancini's is St. Paul's dining room table. It's the city's gathering place, the touchstone for family, business, rotary clubs, government workers, local sports and media celebrities, and the occasional national or international star traveling through town. The restaurant is famous for its steak and for serving a generous portion of pickles and onions prior to the meal.

Mancini's is the working man's special night out. It is a place you can get dressed up to go to, but you can also come in your work clothes, no matter what job you do. At Mancini's, you feel like you're at home. The restaurant is a must-eat destination for anyone in the Twin Cities. It's part of being a resident here. People come not just for the food, but to see the bar and stage as well. They hearken back to a different time and culture, and it's magnificent.

My job at Mancini's was to book entertainment for a Wednesday-night music series. My friends Doug Ruiz and Trixie Goldberg connected me with the job. It was through them that I met Pat Mancini.

It's never easy to follow in the footsteps of a legend. Following Nick Mancini could not have been easy for Pat. I'd never met Nick, so I can't comment on Nick and Pat's relationship in any way. But from what I've seen, Pat's quiet confidence has carried Mancini's over any hurdles that may have come from following in his dad's footsteps.

Pat does everything.

He's in the kitchen helping out when things need to get done quicker and more efficiently. He greets people at the restaurant's entrance. He walks around to all the tables, conversing with his customers and asking them how their food is. He does the same thing in the adjacent bar and music room. He has a job to do. It's his job to be a Mancini. That is a heavy responsibility in St. Paul, and Pat is up to the challenge.

And while the food is terrific, it is not food that brings people back to Mancini's. Nor is it the staff, though they are very strong and loyal, and do a great job. The prices at Mancini's are not as expensive as at other fine restaurants, but they are more than what people expect to pay at Applebee's or Chili's. What brings people back to Mancini's is the substance.

The building itself has significance, and the experience of eating there is far more than what you get at a regular family restaurant. Mancini's has depth, roots, tradition, and opportunities to network, and this perfect combination of elements make a night at Mancini's memorable. Papers and spreadsheets can reveal the length of time this room has been substantial, but numbers, menu choices, and all the other things that form a ledger sheet cannot account for why the restaurant is what it is. That comes down to the Mancini principle.

That comes down to Pat. He legitimately wants to know whether each and every customer is having a pleasurable dining experience. He cares. He cares a lot.

He visits tables and talks to customers. He is thrilled they are eating at his family's restaurant. They are thrilled that the owner came over to check on them. But what the customer is most thrilled about is that Pat Mancini knows them. He notices them. And even if they are only there for the first time, now, they know Pat Mancini. He makes people feel good.

The Mancini name has probably been thrown around in Twin Cities conversations for decades. It is a family to say you know. It will help you if you do. You may not know why, but one thing is certain: it won't hurt you to know the Mancinis. It's like a Char House Ancestry.com that everyone wants to have a link to.

The Mancini principle is also happening at a venue across town called Crooners. In the past few years, Crooners has become a testament to bravery, concept, and old-school methods. Crooners is led by a woman who has committed to her theme.

A few years ago, Mary Tjosvold ("Mary T" to all who know her), along with her husband, now deceased, purchased the old Shorewood Inn building off of Central Avenue and 694 in Fridley. I spent time in that building when it was tragically called the Fridley Crab House, and then again when the name switched to the Shorewood Inn. The transformation of this building fascinates me.

Prior to Mary T, this building belonged to a very well-known Twin Cities restaurant family. This family provided great food and, thankfully, was a champion of local music. They ran multiple venues and provided musicians with work for decades. The Shorewood Inn was one of their venues. A band I started in 2008 called the Irresistibles performed at the Shorewood Inn multiple times.

Back then, the Shorewood Inn was not a popular venue. There was a gigantic bar, like a statement of their priorities, in the middle of the restaurant. And though the room was in the tradition of a 1960s supper club, there was little to no vibe. I believe that was the fault of the Shorewood Inn's leadership at the time.

The Irresistibles was a terrific, soulful band that featured a two-piece horn section, a fantastic rhythm section, and, throughout its iterations, four lead vocalists, including myself and three incredibly powerful female singers named Cate Fierro, Shalo Lee, and Katie Gearty. The band was fresh and funky. We dressed well, and we were welcomed warmly by every venue we performed at, except the Shorewood Inn. The reason for that had nothing to do with numbers, food, booze, or any physical or business attribute. It had everything to do with the restaurant's spirit, vibe, and theme.

When the Irresistibles played at the Shorewood Inn, the feeling in the room was dead. For although they had hired a ten-piece band to perform in their venue, there was nothing coming from the staff and the management, or the audience for that matter, to supersede the feeling that we were a pain in the ass to everyone there.

This amazing band sounded terrible in that room. It was a struggle. The band couldn't hear itself. The singers sang their guts out and couldn't hear themselves. The reaction from the crowd was nonexistent. It is very difficult to perform when you can feel you're unwanted.

The final night we performed at the Shorewood Inn was a particularly difficult night. When it was over, I went to the managers' office to get paid. I then told management I was canceling all our following dates at the venue. They asked why. I told them it was because they hated the band. We could feel it. We could feel that they hated all the band members. It was not worth putting the band through the aggravation for it to always feel this bad. We left. Shortly thereafter, the club shut its doors.

Mary T and Andrew Walesch, Crooners' booking director, who also happens to be an incredible musician and singer, started slowly. They had to take what was given to them and try to make it work. I heard they were doing music in the building, but I had no interest in ever going back there. A couple years into their venture, I was approached by Crooners. They asked me to bring something back to the venue. I agreed to do it.

A few days before my first appearance there, I received an email from Crooners. It said, "We are so excited to host you at Crooners." I read that email, and I was stunned.

It was such a simple and kind thing to say. It was something I had never received from any venue in all my years of performing. I thought it was a brilliant business decision to send this kind of email.

It set the tone. I walked into Crooners for the first time, and it was welcoming. It was warm. It was nothing like the Shorewood Inn. Crooners put the music in the forefront. They didn't treat the band like an annoying afterthought. That was huge.

The simple, old-school hospitality that was core to the Webb Brothers, Mancini's, the Dakota, and Bunker's was now at Crooners. Like the other great venues of Minneapolis, Crooners appreciated their customers and saw the big picture.

Today, Crooners is a nightclub miracle. Artists from around the world come to perform there now. *DownBeat* magazine voted them one of the top jazz venues in the world. Crooners is in Fridley, Minnesota! Did I forget to mention that? Every time I'm on stage at Crooners doing one of the many shows I produce under the Mick Sterling Presents brand, I am so pleased the concept Mary T and Andrew boldly crafted is working so well.

Their theme is music. They pay attention to musicians. They don't speak while musicians are performing. They ask customers to turn off their cell phones. There are no televisions in the room. There is no bar in the room. There are only tables, seats, and the stage. If you are not respecting the musician while they perform, you will be politely asked to leave. They are serious about their theme.

And it works.

People spend a good amount of money for a nice dinner, drinks, and the opportunity to see a great show. Crooners took a gigantic risk. They did not invent their concept; it had been done successfully by the Dakota for decades before them. But the Dakota is a downtown venue. It exists in a different climate, and it has history to lean on.

What Mary T and Andrew did with Crooners was unheard of in this part of the Twin Cities. Every local musician who plays there is grateful for Mary T and Andrew's belief in the scene and for their tenacity to provide this welcoming venue. The Mancini principle strikes again.

My generation loves live music, but we are not going to sit in a bar until 2:00 a.m. every week to see it. We are too old for that. It makes no sense in our lives, nor could we physically do it the way we did in our twenties. We want an earlier show, a great meal, and a great band to watch. And we want to be home in bed before 11:00 p.m. That is the scene now in the Twin Cities, and venues like Crooners, Mancini's, and the Dakota are the champions of this live music methodology.

But the core of their success comes down to how you feel when you're at these venues. Do you feel like your presence is appreciated? Do they care how your experience is? Are their employees happy, and in turn, do they strive to make you happy? Is the food good? Do they care that you enjoy it? Do they show you that they care? Are they committed to providing you a memorable experience?

This is the human stuff the great restaurants seem to do effortlessly. But don't be fooled. It takes a lot of work to look effortless.

Ask. Action. Relief.

It's the First Thing
(Because We've All Been There)

I'm not a huge fan of "hashtag celebrities" who talk a lot then don't do anything tangible about their causes.

It's too easy. A topic they came across made an impression on them, but then, to get a significant amount of praise, they create or share a hashtag about it.

That's not addressing the subject in any real way. It gives nothing of one's self. It's just pressing a button on the shift key and putting letters behind it. It's not nothing; but it ain't something, either.

Locally, I'm somewhat known—for performing, and for being part of organizations and events. On Facebook, I've even been dubbed a "subpar" celebrity. But the one thing no one could call me is a "hashtag celebrity."

In the early 1990s I organized my first benefit as a musician. It was for the St. Joseph's Home for Children in the Twin Cities. As I approached different businesses and individuals about the event, more times than I expected, the people I spoke with already knew me from my performing career. That proved to be quite helpful. Their introduction to me carried with it a certain amount of joy, because they'd seen me perform. That was a good "in" to get them involved with my efforts to help St. Joseph's. For it being my first attempt, the charity event went well. It gave me the spark to try to do more. And I did.

After doing the Heart & Soul concert series to benefit Camp Heartland, I wasn't sure if I wanted to do another event of that size, because, as joyful as it was, behind the scenes, it ended rather painfully. Thankfully, the pain dulled with time, having been initially caused by misconceptions, unwarranted assumptions, and even complete fabrications.

In 2010, I produced a music festival in Excelsior called By the Bay. It featured a collection of great local artists performing in a beautiful setting. During the festival, I was asked multiple times about whom the concert was benefiting. People were used to me doing charity concerts. This particular event was just a music festival, but it certainly got me thinking that perhaps I should organize another benefit.

I spent the following months researching charities, looking for one that really connected with me. Nothing was really hitting the mark. Around that same time, many of my family, friends, and associates were dealing with financial difficulties that they couldn't have planned for. Sometimes, things just happen.

Within a week, I had heard a combination of all their stories. I was intrigued.

What if there was a charity that could help people in such situations, by paying just one bill that came due? That money would be paid directly to the service provider, instead of to the person asking for help. The goal would be to help people within one month of their request, to cover the kind of need that couldn't wait longer than a month. A picture was starting to form inside me.

Eventually, I met with two women who had helped me before with the Heart & Soul events. Cindy Chandler, who is on the board of the Angel Foundation, and Karen Sorbo, who is a nationally renowned live auctioneer, met with me at a café in the Twin Cities. Both of these women are forces of nature.

I told them my idea and the concept for how it would work, and they both thought it was very strong. They each wrote me a check for $300 and urged me to start this charity. That idea became The 30-Days Foundation. Beginning with that meeting, The 30-Days Foundation has become a huge portion of my life.

The 30-Days Foundation was announced in 2010. The second day after I announced the charity, I received the first request for assistance. It came through a Myspace message.

In this message, the woman listed all the assistance she was in need of. It equaled $1,500.00, the maximum I'd said the charity could donate at any one time. But these were the early days, and we didn't yet have $1,500.00 in the account. I noticed, though, that one of her itemized requests was a Sprint phone bill for $78.94. She had included her phone number and account number in her message to us. So, I called Sprint and paid the phone bill.

Within fifteen minutes of her messaging us The 30-Days Foundation had paid her phone bill. Because this was our first donation, I decided to call the woman who asked for our help. I told her we couldn't do the full amount, because we were so brand new, but we'd already paid her phone bill. I told her we hoped it helped.

She then began to sob. They were heavy sobs, like a child's. When she tried to talk, I couldn't understand her.

After she regained her composure, she told me how embarrassed she'd felt, that she couldn't even pay her phone bill. She explained that she'd never had to ask for help before in her life. She hadn't felt comfortable telling her family or friends that she had amassed such debts. We spoke for about fifteen minutes, and I wished her well, and she was very grateful. It was an epiphany phone call.

In the grand scheme of things, $78.94 is not that much money; but that particular $78.94, at that particular time, was everything. It was one less thing for her to worry about. It didn't take care of everything, but at least she knew her phone wasn't going to be shut off. Instead of fourteen things on her plate, she now had thirteen. One less thing.

This was an epiphany moment for me, and for the concept of the charity. It wasn't the amount of the donation that was so important, but the timing of the donation. The donation changed the trajectory for that woman. It gave her a momentary breather and a bit more gumption to try to take care of the other things on her plate.

I was onto something with this concept.

Since that first donation, through to the time you read this story, The 30-Days Foundation will have assisted over one hundred thousand requests to individuals and families in the state of Minnesota. The organization has paid real, glamorous things, like security deposits, first month's rent, back rent, utility bills, medical bills, grocery cards, car repairs, and more. If people fall behind on one or more of these things, that's when things start crumbling. I am very proud of what this charity has accomplished. I'm so grateful we can help people in this way.

For a few years, one of The 30-Days Foundation's efforts was to feed the homeless. We did this in conjunction with great folks from Loaves and Fishes, who shared their food truck with us, and with the help of Serenity Village Church in Crystal, whose members donated hundreds of homemade sub sandwiches each week. We also received weekly food donations from Chipotle, KFC, Leeann Chin, and Holiday stores.

For a few years, The 30-Days Foundation, in conjunction with a young man named Vincent Vera, served hundreds of people per week at the old Dorothy Day Center in downtown

St. Paul. Every Tuesday and Thursday we would serve lunches in the parking lot. It didn't matter how cold it was in the winter, or how steaming hot it was in the summer. We would be there each week. It was a humbling experience, and we were blessed to be able to do it.

As you can imagine, at times it was very stressful to coordinate the logistics of serving many different people. While the vast majority of people we were serving were very grateful for what we were doing, everyone's desperation was evident. And as is true in any situation, some people handle the elements of their misfortune differently. Some handle it with as much kindness and grace as they can. Others have little patience, and let their anger and frustration with their life, and their homelessness, show. They let it be heard to anyone who will listen. That was the situation early one afternoon when I had a revelation in the food truck.

As I looked out, first at some of the people who were there every single week, people who I'm sad to say were "lifers" in this setting, then at the new faces, I realized something.

Everyone we'd been serving these two-plus years had a different reason for why they wound up receiving a free meal from us each week. But the common denominator to all of them is that something had happened. Somewhere along the way, that first thing had happened.

The first thing led to the second, third, and fourth thing, which, eventually, led to the seventh, eighth, and ninth thing, and then there were double digits. And when your misfortunes, those negative things that affect your shelter, your finances, and your personal life, are in double digits, there is a very good chance you'll never dig your way out from them.

But what if you were able to take care of that first or second thing that affected you, before it went down the line to the third, fourth, or fifth thing? What if you were able to get caught up and to get back on track? If that had happened for these people, would they have ended up homeless?

Of course one can't know for sure whether or not they would have, but I think it's safe to say that if someone or something had been able to help them back at that point in their lives, they could certainly have had a better chance at avoiding homelessness. It's not pie-in-the-sky thinking. It's as viable as any other solution being presented, and quite frankly, it's far less expensive and painful for all involved.

In the vast majority of situations, people don't want to be in debt. They want to honor their commitments. Nobody fantasizes about being homeless or unable to pay their bills. It's not a natural human trait.

The 30-Days Foundation provides that breather, so that people in real-life financial crisis can get back on track again. The foundation won't take care of everything, but most people in financial peril don't need everything; they need one or two things, enough to get caught up again.

It works—I see it every day. I'm proud of what the foundation has accomplished, and I'm honored to be able to help.

Because we've all been there.

Algorithms clap on the 1.4 and 3.6. That is the biggest reason I don't trust algorithms. I mean, who the hell can hang with someone like that? Not me, brother, not me.

1 2 3 4

When I was a kid, I took drum lessons from a college student named Dean Discher. I learned how to play the rudiments of drumming from my Haskell Harr books. I spent hours learning how to play five-, seven-, nine-, thirteen-, and seventeen-stroke rolls, paradiddles, double paradiddles, flamacues, and all sorts of other things. I loved playing drums.

As I got older, I started doing theater in junior high and high school. I still played in the school band, but my interest in practicing drums waned. Eventually, I just stopped playing. To this day, I regret never learning how to play a set of drums.

I think if I would've stuck with it, I could have been a respectably good drummer. I have a good sense of rhythm, and I would have been one of those drummers who keeps it simple, which, as a singer, is a style of drumming I've come to appreciate.

Although I am a singer, as a former wannabe rock drummer, I seem to lock into what the drummer is doing first. Initially, I'm more attuned to the drum sounds than I am to the other instruments.

When I write songs, whether I start with melody or lyrics, most of the time I can hear some kind of drum track in my head. I love the drums. I wish I could play them as well as I imagine I could have, but alas, it is not to be. I know I could take lessons and learn. And it would be a story of triumph, if I actually played drums behind a band someday. I should do that, and I could do that, but I know it ain't gonna happen.

A couple of days ago, as I was driving to my morning job at 4:30 a.m., I was listening to the radio. As I accelerated away from a stoplight, I heard the single snare hit of Dylan's "Like a Rolling Stone." It was where it has always been, right where it should be. But for some reason, that day, that snare hit struck me differently.

There are so many memorable moments of drumming in classic rock and R & B songs. There are the moments music fans emulate as they play air drums, and the moments professional drummers practice over and over, striving to duplicate. But in all of rock 'n' roll, has there ever been a moment announcing that everything is about to change as simply and directly as that one particular snare hit?

That snare hit in "Like a Rolling Stone" transformed everything that came after it. It has become the bell continually rung by every popular artist since.

Before that snare hit, songs of that length were never played on radio.

Dylan's lyrics, both in structure and content, were also so original, that while he wasn't remotely similar to those who came before, he influenced everyone who came after. In some way, everyone who followed Dylan, took from Dylan.

Before that snare hit, a vocalist's freedom was strangely limited to their ability to carry a melodic tune. After that snare hit, to stake your claim with your voice, you not only had to be able to carry a tune, but you had to have passion and a distinctive message within that melody.

Before that snare hit, there was an accepted structure of intro, verse one, chorus, verse two, chorus, bridge, chorus. And for the most part, that was just the way things were in any song played on radio. After that snare hit, that structure was no longer gospel. "Like a Rolling Stone" proved it didn't have to be that way.

There is such a wondrous recklessness in this recording. I haven't a clue if it was planned by Dylan, or if it was just this organic thing that happened.

I am not a Dylan scholar, and I'm confident there are millions out there who know more about this song than I do. Millions of words have been written about this song. I'm not breaking any new ground here. I'm just a guy who's heard the song a thousand times, and who, for some reason, was hit by the sound of that snare drum one morning.

I suspect the drummer on that track had no clue that his snare hit would change popular music forever. After all, it was just a drumstick hitting a snare. He had done it a thousand times before. But this one was different, and it's a good thing for all of us that it was.

This song is nearly sixty years old, and every time I hear it, I hear something different. It's such an amazing piece of work. I love that after all these years of playing music, I can still feel a thrill from just hearing moments in particular songs.

"Like a Rolling Stone" is one of those songs. It thrills me. That simple snare hit declared like a cannon that everything was about to change, and we'd all better pay attention.

I love the drums. I always will.

Neglected initial KISS intro:
"You hoped for the best? / You'll hear a band /
The band on stage right in front of you / KISS!!!"

The Best of Bread and Basement Parties

It's funny how memories are triggered, isn't it? They can be triggered by obvious things, or by something so random and unlike the memory itself you wonder how the two can be connected. Today, that random triggering of a memory happened to me.

I am convinced that in every region of this country, people entering adulthood develop their own valid, important rituals. Some may be similar to my own. Others are undoubtedly different, depending on ethnicity, income level, and other factors and circumstances. The only common denominator to these rituals is they happen between the tender ages of thirteen and fifteen, when a person is developing in body, brain, and self-esteem.

mick sterling

For me, there's a song that brings back a ritual of fear, joy, pain, and pleasure from my youth. It coincides with the album *The Best of Bread*, which I first heard at a party in my friend's basement.

From 1974 through 1976, I attended Plymouth Junior High School in Plymouth, Minnesota. Many of my friends from that time can identify with me, as they can also remember the glorious hell that came from playing *The Best of Bread*. They'll remember what it meant to many of us and, certainly, what it meant to me.

You see, junior high was a time of basement parties. They were thrown at various friends' houses.

Some of the basements were in great shape. Some were not. Most of the homes I remember were ramblers. They were single-level homes but had fully furnished basements.

The basement was where we partied. The basement was where we wore Brittania jeans, denim shirts, denim vests, and Flagg Brothers shoes as we faced our fears and fumbled through our feelings for the opposite sex.

I'm sure the basement parties I attended in the seventies were tamer than many of that time. My friends didn't really drink, smoke pot, or drop acid. That wasn't our scene. Most of us were involved in some kind of drama or theatrical performance art, so we had enough fun just exploring each other's remarkable, creative minds and our shared passions for life. Like every teenager, we knew everything.

Our parties would start out rambunctiously, with both sexes talking to each other. But then, the mysterious separation would occur. Boys would be left hanging out with only other boys, while the girls stood around with each other. Elton John, Lynyrd Skynyrd, Zeppelin, Boston, Van Halen, the Beatles, and Simon & Garfunkel would be playing in the background. It was a steady stream of voices, music, and nervousness from both sides.

The girls seemed to hide their nerves better, because they would just talk to other girls to hide their fear. The boys weren't so smart. We showed our nervousness by either acting like an ass or being so painfully shy and awkward that no one would have wanted to be around us. Either way, the roller-coaster dysfunction of being a teenager was on full display at basement parties.

Each party had an early, original flow. As the night progressed, more people would pound down the stairs in their elephant bell-bottoms, puka shell necklaces bouncing against their necks.

As the party progressed, the nervousness would lessen, until finally, someone would conjure up the bravery to talk to the opposite sex.

Then, the party would pivot. The music went into "slow dance" mode. I have no idea who had the insight to manage this shift, but nevertheless, the pivot always happened, and it always seemed to happen at just the right time.

The needle dropped. On came the soft, gentle voice of David Gates. And it was time to get to the real reason you came to the basement party: to try to make out with someone before the night was over and your mom or dad picked you up.

For those of you in my age group who lived where I lived, this was our version of Marvin Gaye's *Let's Get It On*:

"Make It with You"

"Everything I Own"

"Diary"

"Baby I'm-a Want You"

"It Don't Matter to Me"

"If"

"Mother Freedom"

"Down on My Knees"

"Too Much Love"

"Let Your Love Go"

"Look What You've Done"

"Truckin'"

When the needle dropped on *The Best of Bread*, the clumsy sexual ballet began.

Hands that had never touched a girl's hips, or butt, made their debut on whatever body part the girl allowed. The smell of Brut and Old Spice was pungent from the boys. The girls gave off scents of strawberry lip gloss and Babe perfume. Once "Baby I'm-a Want You" came on, the groove really started to develop. The basement would, by then, be filled with teenagers exploring each other in ways that make me uncomfortable to this day.

Kissing happened during *The Best of Bread*. Groping and hugging also happened. In one of these moments, I experienced my first French kiss, which completely freaked me out, because I didn't understand what the hell her tongue was doing in my mouth.

A few seconds later, I got over it, and I clumsily started doing the same to her. Let's just say, this exchange required both of us to reach for a napkin.

By the time the song "Make It with You" started playing, the couples who were going to make out for a long time were off the dance floor, hidden away on some beanbag in a corner of the basement.

But for those of us who, like me, were uncomfortable around girls, that song was also a goal to reach. If you could dance that long with a girl and manage to hide your freight-train-like hormones from showing, if you could keep your cool, you were sitting pretty good. You stood a chance of seeing that girl on Monday and maybe, just maybe, dancing with her again at the next basement party.

Why was *The Best of Bread* the record for us back then? I have no idea, really. It just was.

Where I grew up, that record helped teenagers to reach the next level of intimacy with the opposite sex. It proved to us we stood a fighting chance at overcoming our awkwardness. It taught us how to French kiss. It taught us how to slow dance. It taught us strategy and what to do, and not do, in order to get where we wanted to go.

I have fond memories of that record, though as a teenager, I never purchased it. I only wanted to hear it at a basement party, where I knew someone else was sure to have it.

Someone insulted my jib today.
Nobody insults my jib. Nobody!

Up Periscope

Most of the people who know me these days, outside of my immediate family, know me mainly for my stage persona. When you see someone on stage, your perception of how they got there is probably far more interesting, and far less embarrassing and humiliating, than their actually story is. Because the fact is, embarrassment is the great equalizer. All of us, at some point in our lives, experience mind-boggling humiliation. And it's important. Humiliation has the potential to toughen us up. It's the side of ourselves our friends from youth know, and we can dwell on those embarrassing moments and let them ruin us. Or, we can look back and laugh.

I was thinking today about a particularly bizarre, surreal experience I, along with the entire male population of my junior high school, went through in the 1970s. It happened in Robbinsdale, Minnesota. When I've told people about this, they don't believe it, but I swear it's true.

I'm certain if this happened today, the school would be shut down. Teachers would quit. Administrators would create task forces to deal with the depravity of the situation. Counselors would be on hand for the confused students. Social services would question all the kids who allowed this to happen. The situation I'm speaking of, at the time, seemed perfectly normal. But now, over thirty years away from junior high, I have to wonder how the kids got away with it.

I went to junior high at Plymouth Junior High School in Plymouth, Minnesota. The school was lucky to have a full-size swimming pool. It was considered to be a great facility. Because of the pool, part of our PE requirement was to swim. There's nothing wrong with swimming. It's just the preparation and the curriculum of what we had to do in the pool that are both hysterical and haunting.

The first daunting task was to get nude in the junior high locker room in front of other guys. When you're thirteen-to-fifteen years old, you could be anywhere along the puberty timetable. There were baby-faced, hairless kids alongside fully developed, hairy kids. I think for all of us, it was frightening and humbling at the same time. We were each doing this uncomfortable dance, trying not to look at one another's bodies. From the locker room to the fifteen-minute showers (the gym teachers insisted we be very clean), this teenage freak show was only getting started.

After we rubbed our pale skin raw in the hot, unending, *Silkwood*-esque showers, it was time to enter the pool.

Now, in the normal world, governed by common sense and rationality, people tend to tie tight the drawstring on their swim trunks before they walk into the pool. But as we all know, junior high is not the normal world. It's a twisted, deranged, tangled vortex of shame. But I digress. In that world, we met the upcoming shame fully naked.

As we hung our heads and walked to the pool, we were met with the smell of chlorine and the unwelcome realization that we were the most vulnerable kids in school. Thirty boys in a suburban pool, all of us nude, all of us about to swim nude in front of other boys. Wrap your mind around that for a second. It happened not that long ago, in America.

What was the rationale of the school? Why did they allow this? The teacher said all the loose fabric from swimming trunks would clog the pool's drains. And back then, we believed the teacher's explanation. It made sense to us. And so we lined up at the gym teacher's command, and we proceeded with the swim class.

I now realize the decision to have all the boys swim nude wasn't made by the gym teacher alone. The decision had to come from the school board and superintendent. That makes this monstrosity even more puzzling.

At some point, the proposition had to have been discussed. Someone advocated for nudity among the junior high boys while they swam in front of their teacher and each other. The topic came up, and the school board and superintendent saw logic in the proposal. They voted yes. It made perfect sense to them, and so it must be.

Picture thirty nude teenagers in a row, literally hanging out. The teacher warned us not to create an "up periscope" moment in the pool. We shuddered at the thought, because we all knew our "periscopes" could go up at any time, for no reason at all.

Pick your curse in junior high. Girls start getting their "time of the month." Boys' periscopes go up fifty times a day, without external triggers.

At our teacher's command, we did what he ordered. Swim twenty laps. Swim backstroke for twenty laps. We did what he asked. Those who couldn't complete the tasks were branded failures by the class and were treated differently by the teacher.

In the deep end of the pool there was a diving board. There, things got even weirder.

All of us had to dive. I like to dive. I'm not as big a fan of diving nude, but I wanted to pass the class. We were required to dive to the bottom of the pool to pick up a waterproofed ten-pound brick. Then, we had to swim back to the surface with it.

Some of us were able to swim to the top with that brick. Most of us could not. Our nude bodies propelled to the surface like spastic dolphins. After nearly an hour, our exhausted, chlorine-soaked bodies finally left the pool. We hit the showers for another Chernobyl-worthy scrub-down. We put our

clothes on, left the locker room, and faced the lesser humilia-
tions inherent to junior high hallways.

Did this ordeal make us tougher? Are we stronger men
today for having gone through it? While it's hard to put my
finger on it, I'm confident this experience provided me something: it gave me a humiliation yardstick by which to judge
other, forthcoming, embarrassing moments in my life.

In these days, people are easily offended and ready to sue
over slight inconveniences. My junior high was a different time.
Teachers could intimidate and shame you without risk of being
reprimanded. Parents didn't interfere with what teachers were
doing. In that way, it was a simpler time. I like simplicity, but
my junior high swimming saga was a bit too far for my taste.

Our parents allowed it. No one thought twice about it.
We took it, and all of us survived. The acne all over our bodies
healed. We grew hair where it should be. We graduated, got
married, had kids, got jobs, and lived our lives.

As a parent, you always want your kids to have a better life
than you had. I know this isn't setting the bar very high, but at
least I can say my kids never swam nude in junior high.

Whenever I felt my parenting skills lacking, I was comforted by knowing at least my kids would never have to experience that freshly chlorinated naked hell.

"Get on with it"
        —Marvin Gaye, if he was a
                motivational speaker

The Caffeinated Pageantry

I love the smell of coffee, but honestly, to me, the taste is repulsive.

I have breathed secondhand coffee fumes all my life, and I actually enjoy those quite a bit. Unfortunately, while a spoonful of sugar makes the medicine go down, a pound of sugar, and every sweetener known to man, cannot hide the vile flavor of coffee. For me, there is no escaping it.

One thing I have certainly missed out on is the ceremony and anticipation around the morning's first cup of coffee. There's a caffeinated pageantry millions of people involve themselves in each day, but not me.

I have never known the feeling of a trigger in my brain telling me I require that fix before I can function for the day. I have never known the sensation of the first tentative sip from the aromatic, steaming porcelain or the thermal paper cup.

The first few sips of coffee seem to leave the coffee drinker in a meditative state. It's best to leave them alone for a few minutes while the caffeine and the warmth of the coffee flow through their body. I see it. It looks like a good feeling.

After the initial meditative state, coffee drinkers start to come to life.

If you're with someone who's made a pot of coffee, what follows is, to me, the best reason to drink coffee—conversation over coffee.

Coffee is a common denominator between people. Over coffee, people share stories about work, family, and personal issues. I used to see people smoke cigarettes while they drank their coffee. I don't see that much anymore.

Although I would rather drink a condensed liquid brick than a cup of coffee, I often find myself in Dunn Brothers or Caribou, coffee shops that are quite popular in the Twin Cities, as I do work for my band or for The 30-Days Foundation.

Coffee is why you come to these places, but they are far more than that. They are the gathering space for the neighborhood.

Coffee shops are one of the few places young teenagers can hang out. They are a place for people who work from home to hold business meetings, so they don't have to bring others into their messy house.

If you have a laptop and a cell phone, why even pay for office space? You can sit at a table in your nearby coffee shop and run your international business. The coffee shop is a place filled each day with confessions, business, lies, and half-truths.

I enjoy the atmosphere, though I can't complete the final, liquid transaction of drinking coffee.

As an observer in the coffee-obsessed world, I have some comments, and recommendations.

If you are one of those people who likes black coffee to be weak, save yourself the potential ridicule from the teenager behind the counter. Make your coffee at home, visit the lower level of a Lutheran church, or go see a friend who's in the hospital; you'd be better served.

You can almost feel the sympathy and scorn from baristas when you order a drink far beneath what they're capable of preparing. You are among the dying breed of Americans who consume coffee because it's what adults do. You are out of place in these shops. You're Wang Chung at Coachella. Save your Folgers and Hills Bros. coffee tins. Put them in your backyard for target practice. We will miss you when you are gone.

If you are over the age of fourteen, and you order a fruit smoothie, you should not be allowed to remain in a coffee shop. If you must order it, do so, and get out.

A grown person ordering a fruit smoothie has no place in a coffee shop.

That is why God gave inspiration to some guy named Julius to create the tangy, tongue-tingling sensation that is Orange Julius.

A scone is a worthless piece of pastry. I am confident nobody really likes a scone. They just order one because it gives them a sense of internationalism. You live in America, dammit!

Order a muffin, preferably a blueberry muffin. You can stay if you order a muffin (or, if you must, a scone). But you cannot stay as long as someone who orders coffee.

One cold, rainy, blustery day last week, I was in line behind a woman who ordered a small decaf sugar-free latte with skim milk. I felt pity for this woman when I heard her order.

Why would she go out on a terrible morning like this to order that drink?

Wouldn't it have been easier for her to stay in her pajamas and microwave skim milk? Why go to a coffee shop to order something like that? If that kind of coffee is a highlight in her day, it is time to find a pill instead.

The coffee world is a world I will never truly understand. Sure, I can order a hot chocolate and sit with you while you drink your coffee, but in the end, to me, it's all a sham.

Even something as mechanical as going to the coffee shop every day should, at its core, have soul. I will never know the feeling coffee brings you. I have a soul, just not, I suppose, a caffeinated one.

Remember when you're feeling under-used,
you're really never as under-used as Taylor Swift
was on "Half of My Heart" by John Mayer.

Toasted, Nicely Toasted

The creation of the perfect piece of toast is a challenge men all over the world have struggled to conquer. Women have figured out mysteries like these long ago. But for men, the quest to create the perfect piece of toast is one that is as frustrating as the game of golf.

In golf, for example, occasionally your swing, your follow-through, and the heavens all align to give you the perfect shot. On the very next hole, you revert to old habits and you want to throw your clubs in the drink. Making toast, like golf, is a delicate dance composed of persistence, patience, attention to detail, and a keen sense of knowing when enough is enough.

It is not unlike wooing a woman. It requires forethought and cunning.

Though you have all the tools to make toast, sometimes the results will be unsatisfactory. To quote an old cover by Southside Johnny and the Asbury Jukes, "It ain't the meat, it's the motion."

The choice of bread is the first crucial step.

For grilled cheese or peanut butter and jelly sandwiches, white bread, even Wonder Bread, will suffice. But just like SpaghettiOs, white bread only tastes good to younger taste buds.

As you grow up, your senses and tastes become more refined. You want more from life, which in turn, means you expect more from your toast. But what are you doing to create that tasty, improved toast you're ready to bite into? As with most things, it takes more than one element to attain a successful resolution.

How long you let the bread stay in the toaster is a perplexing part of the process.

The average person would tell you to just set the dial to a certain level. Those people are so sure they're correct, they actually think that simple motion will eliminate toast problems. I pity those people.

Every man knows that you have to stand over the toaster and watch your toast. You need to press the lever down and watch the toast pop up, checking to see if it's the right color over and over again until it's perfect.

If you're alone, you stand a better chance of attaining the perfect golden glow on those two slices (or four, if you come from a family of means that has a four-slice toaster). But if the phone rings, or your dogs have to go outside, it can throw that split-second timing off, leaving you with well-done toast that is beneath your dignity to consume.

When you make toast, all things must take a back seat. Your friends, phone calls, job, marriage, kids, pets, and everything else must be paused for the sake of your toast.

The next step is choosing the right knife to spread your topping of choice.

A butter knife always does the job, but sometimes, a butter knife isn't around. Sometimes it's a steak knife, fork, spoon, or, on rare and desperate occasions, a spatula.

The vast majority of us don't have the talent to improvise with a spatula. Most men are butter knife men. We're simple folk with simple needs. Men, for God's sake, come prepared. Do the dishes so you can have at least one clean butter knife when needed.

All that's left is butter. Sweet, sweet butter! Cow's gift to man.

In the supermarket, it takes a form that is a little hard and distant from us. It is wrapped up tightly in annoying wax paper that is hard to take off. But with some time in a warm cupboard, butter reveals its softer, friendlier, and easier side. It becomes an approachable substance, almost encouraging us to find out more about it.

If your toast is done and the butter is too hard, only bad things come of it.

The bread breaks. The butter clumps. It won't spread evenly over the toast. Sure you can eat it, but inside you're disappointed.

You've let yourself down. You know how to do it and you blew it. Sure your stomach is full after you eat it, but it's a hollow victory. You don't brag about it to your friends. You keep it inside. It festers until you have another opportunity to make toast.

When that happens, you have to dig down deep and remember the basics: timing, preparation, attention to detail, common sense, and complete concentration on the task at hand.

The butter, bread, knife, toaster, and plate . . . every man has these things, but it takes more than this to make toast. You must visualize the result, and act to make it happen.

Your plate, correct knife, and warm, spreadable butter should all be within reach the split second that toast springs from the toaster. If those important elements are not within reach and in your control, the result will be an abyss of burnt toast and chunks of hard butter.

Perfectly colored buttered toast is one of life's sweetest things. It offers small adventures in the form of additions: peanut butter, honey, bananas, jelly, or the Xanadu of perfect toast, cinnamon sugar.

In the hard world we live in, men shouldn't even try making cinnamon toast. Only moms, grandmas, and girlfriends or wives who really love you can make cinnamon toast. A perfect piece of toast can give a man the will to carry on. It has, many times. The promise of Neil Armstrong's wife to make him cinnamon toast if he successfully landed on the moon and got his butt back to Earth is actually the key reason we landed on the moon. Ask NASA—it's true.

This noble pursuit of preparing and consuming the perfect piece of toast is a lifelong quest, one worth attempting by all men. For women, attaining this goal is not so significant; making perfect toast is simply in their DNA, like knowing when guys aren't telling the truth.

Women know how the butter spreads.

They know how to work the knife.

They know what the knife is supposed to do and how it should be properly navigated.

They know how to tell that bread who's boss.

Honestly, women have no need for toast in their lives. They could survive without it. They just make it occasionally to show men how it's done.

In the end, women know that slices of perfect toast are like men, expendable. Neither is necessary, but they are both nice to have around when needed.

Toilet tissue is trying to purchase
humans now, just to get back at us.
We had it coming, though, so I get it.

Fear, Respect, and Selflessness

In the years to come, when the COVID-19 pandemic is behind us and we have forged a new "normal," I'm sure we'll commiserate about what we've all been through. Depending on whom you speak to, the stories about it will vary wildly.

For many, this stressful time has brought personal and professional discoveries, and creative victories. But there have also been significant, painful shortfalls. Heavy prices were paid, not just physically, but mentally, and for some people, these struggles have touched the very core of whom they are and whom they've had to become to get through this.

I have found that fear cannot be negotiated with.

I don't negotiate with it; it's a waste of my time. I'll lose, and I don't like to lose. Fear has all the answers and can even make sense of the most preposterous hypothetical scenarios. Fear explains things in a calm, rational way.

However, I have respected COVID-19 because it's obviously a real thing. To dismiss it as a fraud is just not genuine or true. But respecting something and fearing something are two dramatically different routes to take.

I have chosen to respect it, not fear it. I've found ways to live my life within the strange parameters of the COVID-19 era, while still being respectful of those who are in fear of it. It's a delicate and frustrating tightrope to walk in my day-to-day life.

Among the many sad things that are happening during this pandemic is the lessening, and sometimes complete elimination, of human touch. We cannot readily hold hands, hug, kiss, or partake in all the natural human behaviors that usually bind loved ones. It's particularly sad and painful to witness the ways this affects our senior loved ones in assisted-living homes. As I enter my sixtieth year of life, I am not that far behind them, and those in my age tribe are all going through what I am with their own loved ones.

The woman named Neva, who is, thankfully, my mom, has now been in an assisted-living setting for the past few years. For a woman of her age, she is mentally sharp and physically fit, which bodes very well for me and my siblings as we approach her stage of life.

Through the pandemic, Mom has had to endure quarantine and isolation per the safety guidelines of where she lives.

Mandates and rules are everywhere in our lives, and this is especially true for seniors who require extra protection. I'm not completely convinced the route we've taken has been effective. These methods seem drastic to me. They put connection, touch, hugging, and face-to-face contact in the background at best. It's deflating and heartbreaking for all involved, but this is what has been set up by those in charge, and there's really not much I can do about it. Maybe that is why, in these hard times, the unexpected moments of kindness and selflessness are giving me so much hope.

In a phone conversation with my mom a few weeks ago, she shared with me that recently she had to leave her home to get some errands done. She took the bus provided by the care facility. During her errands, she found herself in the city where she'd raised all of us. The bus driver inquired, "Neva, isn't your home around here?" To which my mom stated that it indeed was. The driver, without prompting, got the address from my mom and eventually parked in front of her old house.

My mother purchased that home in 1966. She was a single mom with four kids. She received no financial support from my father, and she worked as a waitress in a local nightclub to make ends meet. The house was in horrendous shape in 1966. She paid $14,000 for it. This house got us out of living with the lovely Tanner family, who had a similar rambler a couple of blocks away. They also had four kids of their own, and their house was bursting at the seams with us there. We were so grateful to be at this new house, despite its condition. Eventually, with all our love, the house blossomed. My sister Jessica moved in a few years later, and Mom married Carroll Wickstrom, a man who provided her comforts and experiences she never would have had without him. She hated leaving that house, but she knew she had to, because at their late age, it just wasn't safe for either one of them to be there anymore. Beautiful, but hard stuff.

The bus driver then proceeded to get off the bus and walk up to the front door to knock. No one answered. Mom was waiting in the bus during this. As he walked down the driveway, he asked Mom to get out of the bus so they could take a look around the outside of the house. And she did!

They saw the garden she spent decades tending. She saw the back deck where she'd spent so many seasons in Minnesota. She saw her beautiful backyard and so many things she thought she'd never see again. As my mom told me this on the phone, I was getting choked up, because I knew what it meant to her, and also to me. I started blubbering. But I was also so blown away by the amazing selflessness and kindness of this bus driver who went out of his way to do this for Mom.

She then told me the bus driver asked if there were any neighbors she wanted to see while they were there. He proceeded to knock on one neighbor's house, but no one was there. Then he tried a second door. This one belonged to our long-ago neighbor Diana. Mom waited near the bus.

As Diana opened the door, she greeted the bus driver. Then she saw Mom near the bus and screamed, "Neva, my God, I thought I'd never see you again." She was crying happily, as this was the first time she'd seen Mom in years. They then proceeded to catch up with each other for the next twenty minutes, loving every instant that was happening between them.

In normal times, this would have been accompanied by a long hug and kisses on the cheek, but due to COVID-19, this beautiful human interaction happened within social distance regulations. It doesn't lessen the impact of this beautiful moment, but it certainly dictated the physicality of their meeting. But hell, I'll take it. Without this man's kindness, this would have never happened at all.

As I was sobbing on the phone, I started wondering something. I asked Mom if it was customary for only one person to be on the bus at a time for local errands. She told me she wasn't alone on that bus; there were others on the bus who watched the two of them catch up. That's when the story came full circle for me.

I can't even fathom how much each and every person on that bus wished they could have been in my mom's place, seeing their old neighbors, and seeing the homes they'd left behind, the homes they'd raised their children in. The thought of it is so beautiful.

The kindness shown by this bus driver, who by all rights should be burned out from doing the job he does every day, was remarkable. I don't know if it's the safest thing in the world to do during the pandemic, but I know Mom stayed safe during this, and I'm forever grateful for what happened.

My mom saw her house one more time. She saw her neighbor one more time. This was a very good day, and it's good for all of us to cherish these days when they happen.

Seven trillion elephants swimming in pudding. That sentence has never been uttered or written in the history of the world.

Dumbo ... Dumbo ... Dumbo!

We are a country in ideological and economic turmoil right now. Is there anything everyone can agree on? Can anything bring this wounded country together? Is there one thing that can reduce anyone, with any heart at all, to tears? One word is all that's needed to bring this country some comfort: *Dumbo*.

There can be no debate, *Dumbo* is the greatest, saddest Disney film of all time.

Disney has made many films that are more popular than *Dumbo*. Many have made far more money. Some are more stunning stylistically. *Dumbo* wasn't made using computer technology; the film is too old. Yet, it is the best film Disney ever made.

My experience with *Dumbo* began when my kids were babies.

We had a videotape of a Disney TV program someone recorded for us. On this tape, there were a few short cartoons. There was a Disney version of *Jack and the Beanstalk* with Mickey Mouse as Jack paired against some dopey giant. It's great. The other short cartoon was *Lambert the Sheepish Lion*. This is about a lion who's raised by sheep. He doesn't realize he's a lion. He doesn't know he has the ability to be ferocious, until all his sheep friends are threatened by the slobbering wolf. Again, I loved it. The last short was *Ferdinand the Bull*. Ferdinand is the biggest bull in Mexico, but all he wants to do all day is smell flowers. Spectacular. Once I got through all of those, it was time for *Dumbo*.

The film begins with the late, great Sterling Holloway, the voice behind Winnie the Pooh, *The Jungle Book*'s Kaa, and so many other beloved Disney characters. In *Dumbo*, he's the stork, about to deliver Dumbo to an expectant mother elephant on a circus train.

It seems to take a very long time before Jumbo, Dumbo's mother, receives her baby from the stork, but eventually she does.

Once Jumbo arrives, all of the other busybody elephants *ooh* and *ahh* at how cute Dumbo is wrapped up in his blanket. If you've seen the film, you've got to admit that Dumbo is the sweetest, most lovable of all Disney characters. Yes, this includes Bambi and Thumper (I know what you're thinking out there, but my feelings are very strong about this).

The first pivotal moment comes when Dumbo's blanket opens, revealing his huge ears. The other elephants are shocked and horrified. Dumbo's mother looks at him and doesn't see anything wrong with him. He's her baby and that's all that matters. Moms are great that way. I was a new parent once; I understand this moment.

By today's standards, *Dumbo* is politically incorrect and racist. It's not quite *Song of the South*, but it's certainly in the parking lot, waiting to get in.

The first racist moment comes when the fantastic singing circus train halts. The circus workers, called roustabouts, do their thing. They're all African-American men (animated men, of course, for the sake of clarity), and the song they sing is similar to old spirituals, but if you listen to the lyrics, they tell another story completely. Let's put it this way: Disney could not make *Dumbo* today with that scene and that song. It happens again later in the film when Dumbo meets the crows. They sing their wonderful song, "When I See an Elephant Fly." The crows' portrayal is supposed to emulate African-Americans of that period, and it's deeply uncomfortable to watch, because it's so wrong in so many ways. Still, I'm glad *Dumbo* wasn't banned like *Song of the South* was, but I could certainly see it happening someday.

Everybody makes fun of Dumbo because of his ears. He's a freak to the other animals in the circus. When he's paraded through the town where the traveling circus is performing, he trips and falls repeatedly over his own ears. Everybody laughs at Dumbo, but he remains sweet and lovable.

Once back at the circus, an incredibly ugly, mean kid grabs at Dumbo and tries to humiliate him. That sets his mother off. Never mess with a mother's little boy. As the son of an Italian mother, I know, it's just not done.

This kid crosses the line, and Dumbo's mom gives him a swat with her trunk. That sets a bunch of things in motion and gets her in trouble. She winds up locked away in a separate boxcar, apart from the other elephants and, more importantly, from Dumbo.

Then comes the part that destroys me. I've probably seen this film fifty times, and it still gets me. While Dumbo's mom is locked up, the circus's ringmaster decides to have Dumbo work with the clowns. It's a huge embarrassment for the regal elephants. So much so, in fact, that the elephants decide Dumbo is no longer a pachyderm.

He's humiliated, tired, and very lonely for his mother. Dumbo's only friend is a savvy, entrepreneurial mouse. This mouse sees how sad Dumbo is and tells him he knows where his mother is locked up. Dumbo cheers up, and together they start their journey to see Dumbo's mom.

When Dumbo arrives at a solitary boxcar under a moonlit sky, he sees his mother's trunk poking out of the bars. She knows he's there. Dumbo walks up to the boxcar, and his mother cradles him with the lower portion of her trunk. Just then, the song "Baby Mine" plays as Dumbo's mom starts swinging Dumbo back and forth. As she sings, a huge tear wells up in Dumbo's eye. The tear falls down his trunk, and he starts crying.

At this point, I'm done. I'm a puddle. It's embarrassing, but I can't help myself. Dumbo and his mom are back together again, if only for a while. They love each other so much. Hell, I'm tearing up right now just writing this.

The rest of the song features other animals in the circus with their babies. They're cute, I get it, but it pales in comparison to Dumbo and his mom.

As the song ends, Dumbo and his mouse friend have to depart. As they walk away, his mother waves with her trunk, not knowing if she'll ever see him again. I'm always glad when that scene is over. Not because I hate the scene. On the contrary, I just can't handle anything sadder than that.

Of course, the rest of the film is filled with fantastic images: the psychedelic "Pink Elephants on Parade," and the scene with the crows wherein Dumbo realizes he can fly . . . In my estimation, *Dumbo* is much sadder and more touching than *Bambi*, or any other Disney film. Dumbo is down, but he never gives up. The people who are mean to him eventually realize how special Dumbo is. His mother loves him. He has a friend to support him. He wins in the end. What's not to love about that?

Dumbo is very special to me and my kids. I'll watch it anytime, anywhere. If it starts, I have to watch the whole film, even though I've seen it so many times. It's so sad and beautiful.

Find *Dumbo*. If you have it already, watch it again. If you have kids, you've probably seen it as many times as I have. It doesn't matter. Watch it again.

In these times of so much conflict and tension, it's nice to just lose yourself for a while and root for a funny-looking little "pack-eee-derm" who eventually triumphs. It gives us all hope.

Neuroscientists have just announced that despite repeated statements through history, nothing is actually based on Homer's Odyssey.

Larry's Last Hurrah

I used to be a news junkie. CNN, FOX, BBC, MSNBC, *Meet the Press*, *The McLaughlin Group*. I could never get enough. My viewing habits have changed quite a bit, but I still like to be on top of current events. These networks and their online resources keep me up to date.

However, when watching these shows, I also notice a great deal of pomposity and long-winded questions and comments from the hosts. I am thinking specifically of one of the great hosts who retired a few years ago, Larry King.

In general, I feel the reporters and announcers have forgotten that they are not news; their job is to report the news.

Even when an announcer states his or her personal opinion on a topic, the topic is the star. Some members of the media seem to think they are more interesting than the actual news they are telling us. The tele-journalists' promotion of their own personal thoughts has reached red-hot levels on both sides of today's political spectrum. It's got me thinking about Larry King. If he were on the air today, how would he handle the biggest stories hitting his news desk?

Let's say there was absolute, undeniable proof that Jesus Christ had come back to earth, ready to show his face and make his first statement to the world. Since he has seen everything we have done since the crucifixion and resurrection, he is not only incredibly durable, but also media savvy. Thus, he has chosen to make his statement on the most-popular worldwide cable station, CNN. Specifically, he's decided to appear on *Larry King Live*.

A one-on-one with our nightly last man in suspenders. Jesus would arrive in New York City, in person, in a limo provided by CNN. Donkeys just don't get the job done anymore, but perhaps New Yorkers could still wave palm fronds as he passes; what good are palm fronds to us in the twenty-first century, anyway? Think of it, the Son of God, Jesus Christ, on television. How would it be handled?

VOICEOVER: This is CNN, and now, *Larry King Live*.

LARRY KING: Hello, this is Larry King reporting live from New York City. I don't have to tell any of you in the viewing audience tonight this is a big night. Not just for the United States, but for the world. Not just for Christians and Jews, but for all religions.

We in the media pretend to be unfazed by our celebrity and political guests. Honestly, while they may be impressive, they are, ultimately, people, like you and me.

We go about our jobs each day and deliver the news to you. Tonight is not one of those normal nights. Tonight is bigger. It's safe to say that the producers of this show have done a bang-up job and booked the biggest guest to ever grace my set here at CNN. Tonight's guest is more popular than Gloria Allred.

Before I introduce our guest, let me tell you a story about when I sang a duet with Joey Bishop and Peter Lawford at the Sands Hotel and Casino in Las Vegas.

I was sitting with Angie Dickinson and Shelley Winters watching the show, when Joey called me up on stage. I was frozen in fear. Angie nudged me. Shelley picked me up from my chair and escorted me to the stage. As I stepped on the stage, the orchestra played the familiar refrain of "Come Rain or Come Shine."

There I was on stage, the skinny kid raised on the streets of New York City, singing in Las Vegas with Joey Bishop and Peter Lawford. It was magical. I felt like a god. Our next guest is familiar with being thought of in that way.

Momentarily, you will be witnessing the biggest moment in television history. But before that happens, have I told the story of how my nine-year-old son was cheated out of a victory in his Little League game the other day?

I was in the stands with my lovely wife when I witnessed this miscarriage of justice. My boy was picked off at first base.

It was clear he was safe. The first baseman was a cheater, along with his entire team and coach.

But I could see the umpire was not going to change his mind, so I jumped off the bleachers and confronted the umpire. I got right in his face and he got in mine.

He didn't seem to care about my celebrity status—his mind was made up. As I was reaching my fever pitch of anger, a voice whispered inside my head and said, "Larry, calm yourself, this isn't right." I felt a presence.

It was as if somebody were watching me, looking out for me, if you will, telling me there's another way to deal with this situation. It gave me a lot of peace. Our guest tonight states he provides peace. It took a very long time to get him here, but tonight, we have him.

Before he joins us, I want you to consider a few things.

Have you ever wondered why Montreal had a Major League Baseball team? Can you name one player on the Expos?

Has there ever been a better sandwich than the one I got on Chicago's Michigan Avenue on a hot summer day in 1973?

Will the cast of *B.J. and the Bear* ever reunite? Whatever happened to that chimp? The one I loved . . . I don't think that chimp would rip my face off. Not THAT chimp. It's amazing what animal trainers can do these days, isn't it?

Is Jennifer Aniston destined to live her life alone after divorcing Brad Pitt? Is there something wrong with the men in her life, or is it her?

So many things happen every day, and even a network as large as CNN can't see everything.

Our next guest doesn't have that problem. He claims to be able to see everything. He has suffered immeasurable pain, sacrificed everything, forgiven everyone, and, at the same time, provided an overabundance of joy and hope to many people.

Gossip and innuendo have followed him from the start. Books have been written about him. Films have been made about him. Yet people never seem to tire of him. As a matter of fact, the book in which he is prominently featured, the New Testament, published by Doubleday, is in many ways the *Dark Side of the Moon* of publishing. People just can't get enough of this man.

How does he handle the stress?

Look at the struggles of Lindsay Lohan, Britney Spears, the Jonas Brothers, and the Kardashians. Watch how they cope with paparazzi and fame. Young kids have to put up with so much these days. But if you're going to be in this business, if you want to succeed, you have to accept the fact that you are public property. The public made you, and the public can tear you down. Our guest is not unfamiliar with that concept—he has firsthand testimony to prove it. Luckily for us, we have him here tonight.

Ladies and gentlemen, for the first time in the history of worldwide broadcasting, it is my distinct honor to introduce, from the village of Nazareth, the carpenter-turned-savior, the Son of God, Jesus Christ.

JESUS CHRIST: Thank you, Larry. It's wonderful to be here.

LARRY KING: Jesus . . . uh . . . Mr. . . . umm . . . Christ . . . uh . . . Jesus Christ, I'm sorry, but we're up against a hard break, plus we have live helicopter footage of a car chase on the 101. But we thank you so much for making the time to show up, and we wish you well on your travels.

Coming up next, from *The View*, the consistently insightful and hilarious Joy Behar speaks with me about her opinions on those who give opinions differing from her own.

Optimism and hope are not the cloak of the naive. Don't let anyone take that away from you.

What Is Yours to Give

The act of giving yourself to God is a deeply personal decision. Each person gives in a deeply personal, unique way. And while there are certain accepted tenets to uphold, and physical structures to walk inside of, there is certainly more than one way to give yourself to God.

Some folks participate in weekly televised gatherings that number in the tens of thousands in attendance. Often, the preachers at these events have many possessions, more even than their followers could possibly conceive of having.

I won't make a blanket accusation of preachers who are clearly making millions from their message; it still comes down to whether you believe what they are saying or not.

I don't begrudge them living lavishly. For some reason I don't really understand, it doesn't bother me.

It's not something I would do. I think it's garish and goes against the message, but if the followers of these preachers aren't bothered by it, if they are all right with making these preachers richer, it's their personal decision.

It's not the same as their decision to give their lives to God, but the principle is in the same ballpark. After all, the riches these preachers amass stem from the words that come out of their mouths. People who are moved enough by those words give of themselves financially to continue to hear the words each week.

I started reading the Bible a few years ago. I didn't read it every day. I know I should have, but I didn't. I keep thinking I want to start again, but as of this time, I still haven't picked it up to read it in full.

There are some things I understand, and some I don't. It has given me great comfort at times, and other times, it's left me in states of boredom, confusion, understanding, and awe. Maybe I'm not alone in that reaction.

There have been periods in my life when I've attended a church steadily, and for the most part, it hasn't gone too well.

I would find myself unable to focus on what the pastor was saying. Most of the time, it's because I just wasn't moved. Maybe it would have been completely different if I had gone to a Baptist church with incredible, uplifting, emotional gospel music, but that was not the kind of church I went to as a child.

When I was a child, our priest bored me to tears. The church was actually in a gymnasium. It wasn't a tradition-al-looking church, so in my child-brain, I just didn't get it. I couldn't wait to get out of there. I wasn't listening to anything being said. It was just keeping me away from the McDonald's lunch I knew I'd get that afternoon. It just didn't work for me.

Later in my life, I attended a church in the Twin Cities that was creating a lot of spiritual excitement in town. It incorporated a fully realized music portion with a large amount of very accomplished singers. The pastor had a very charismatic personality, and the parking lot filled beyond capacity every time he was scheduled to speak.

When I started attending this church, they were in the process of raising funds. They wanted to build an extremely ambitious campus to serve as the headquarters for all their mission work. It was a grand plan, and it was very impressive. I had no doubt the campus would get finished, and everything the pastor said would eventually happen there, would get done.

While I attended, a significant portion of each service was focused on the building of the campus: what it was going to enable, and what was needed financially to make the campus a reality. The campus was a necessity, because the mission needed more space to handle what was happening within the church. But while appreciating the beautiful efforts being done to create this campus, I couldn't get past the fact that in all the times I attended this church, it was seldom even half-full. I couldn't get past the recurring thought as to the futility of building a much-larger campus when the church couldn't fill the one it had.

As soon as I came to grips with that, everything said by this very talented pastor and his assistant were over my head. I believed they were men of God. I felt they were speaking truth, but not unlike my earlier experience as a child, it was evident to me that all of it was lost on me.

It concerned me then, and it still concerns me to this day. Why, when others were so moved by the words and music within that church, was I, for the most part, uninspired and inattentive? Am I not fully giving myself to the Word, or am I purposely blocking it for some reason?

The Old Testament doesn't move or inspire me. It is filled with stories of great beauty and great cruelty, and it's very interesting, but the words aren't words that motivate me or make me want to know more about God, even though I believe them to be factual. The first time I read passages from the Old Testament, it felt like a collection of adventure stories. Saying that, I understand they are, according to the Bible, a "cornerstone" of everything that happens later in the New Testament. Still, the Old Testament doesn't do it for me. Now, I understand "doing it for me" is not the intent of the Old Testament. But the words of the Old Testament, while beautiful and magnificent in scope and depth, are, for many people, an insurmountable hurdle.

The fantastic wonder of Genesis, Sodom and Gomorrah, the Tower of Babel, Noah's Ark, Adam and Eve, Moses, Joshua, King David, Solomon, Job, and all the others . . . I believe it all happened—if not exactly as written, then very close to it.

The words within these stories are filled with beauty, but also with anger and death. In the Old Testament, God, while loving and generous, was also jealous and vengeful. It's the jealous and vengeful God many people can't get past.

How can you love a God who is so jealous and angry, who has been documented in the Bible to end life, in the most horrific of ways, for those who didn't follow His word?

I want to learn more about God and Jesus Christ. However, I am less inclined to learn about God when I'm in large groups or organized settings. One of the main reasons is the music. Music is such an important aspect of church. A healthy portion of church funds goes to providing music that will impact and inspire churchgoers. For me, the music is unsatisfying.

When I hear music at churches, the performer and singer-songwriter aspect of my personality keeps getting in the way of the message.

It's like going to a restaurant with my mom, the former server and restaurant manager. She's too inside. She knows how things should work, and when they don't, she can't enjoy the experience as much. She doesn't enjoy the dining experience as much as someone who isn't entrenched in the restaurant industry, because she doesn't think like a regular customer. She knows too much, so her tendency is to critique instead of purely enjoy.

I feel the same way when I hear the majority of church song performances. They are certainly done earnestly and with emotion. They are purely performed. None of that is my critique. Even the quality of the singers and musicians doesn't really bother me. What bothers me is the length of the songs. They just go on too long.

I'm confident that if instead of being seven-to-ten-minute songs, church songs packed all their content into a sweet two-minute-forty-five-second-to-three-minute period, these songs would move me, because I would have greater respect for the songwriting craft that achieved its message in this compact time frame. I'm not saying this type of thought is correct, but it's what I always come back to.

In my estimation, the best music about God comes from Bob Dylan's two records *Slow Train Coming* and *Saved*.

Those songs affect me. Songs like "I Believe in You," "What Can I Do for You," or "Are You Ready" are so direct in their messaging, I completely trust his belief in what he is singing.

While I know there are incredible gospel and faith-based artists who do wonderful work, I've just felt as much impact from them as I do when listening to Otis Redding sing "These Arms of Mine," Aretha singing Marvin Gaye's "Wholy Holy," or anything by Ray Charles that touches and moves me. Those are the artists whose songs bring me closer to Christ.

Here is what I do know. I know the comfort and solace God provides. I know God guides those who choose to believe in Him.

I know God is someone who shows love to those who ask for love to be shown. I know God puts people in your life for a reason.

I know I'm in this world to make a difference. I know prayers work: for yourself, and when you pray for others. I know Jesus Christ is the Son of God. I've been told God knows everything we're doing, because our lives have already been planned by Him. That one I'm still trying to wrap my head around, but I do believe things happen for a reason.

I don't require a large group of people to validate my beliefs. These things don't require the approval of others.

Frankly, I think a considerable number of people who attend church for a long time unintentionally begin perceiving other members of their church in a way that makes them comfortable, instead of perceiving members as they truly are: humans who, at times, have frailties and flaws and need the grace that Jesus asks us to provide others.

Maybe because it's such a personal thing, I don't want to be judged by others for how I live my life with God. How can someone fully relate to my feelings about God, when everyone has a different relationship with God in the first place? I have the utmost respect for people who live their lives differently than mine, but I don't feel compelled to emulate their ways in my life with Jesus. I'm sure there are some people out there who have some things to say about that.

I certainly recognize the power of fellowship, and what can happen within a church when that fellowship is all united. Maybe my lack of attendance at church means I need someone new to inspire me.

Or perhaps I need to start reading the Bible some more and find some new things to inspire me. Perhaps I need to downsize and find a group of people to discuss things with. There must be some other option for me.

It seems self-serving to read the Bible just to find ways to validate any guilty or bad feelings that may come my way. I also don't want to read the Bible because it's expected of me to do so. I should read the Bible because it's something I want to do in my life on this earth. I should read it because it's what people who believe do. I do believe, but I haven't done this yet. I have to work on this.

We have been given one life, and that life is breathtakingly short. I'm too familiar with this, sometimes.

I would like this life to be one of opportunities and accomplishments that come from the one man who gave everything that could be given of himself. It's up to me to use what was given to me, and in this way, I can honor the gift.

I'm trying.

Your day would be much better if you would just accept that you don't know what the word "malware" means too, instead of just nodding your head like you do when someone brings it up in conversation. You don't know. It's alright if you don't know. You can't know everything.

You're My Friend, Right?

There are multiple simple truths in life. As with all simple truths, you can either embrace them, or ignore them. As I've grown older, I've found that the sooner I'm able to accept simple truths, the better off I am.

One simple truth I accepted long ago is that as a musician, it is impossible to be liked by everyone.

I didn't like accepting that truth, because I'm not a confrontational person. I want to be liked by everyone. If someone is mad at me, I want to find out why. If someone thinks I've done something against them, I want to find out why. I'm not a person who is comfortable knowing someone out there doesn't like me, or even hates me. Some people are comfortable in that skin, I'm not.

I recently came across a Facebook post that intrigued me.

It was from a person who had apparently just released a project he had been working on for years.

On the post, he said he no longer wanted to hear negativity or criticism about his work. If he did, he said he would unfriend the negative person. When I read this, I commented, telling him he was in the wrong business if he was going to try to surround his world with zero criticism. I was encouraging him to be strong, have faith in his own work, and not worry about negative people. A few minutes later, he deleted the entire post, and now it's nowhere to be found. I shook my head.

The creation of music is such a deeply personal thing. It doesn't matter if it's an instrumental, or a song with lyrics. If it comes from your gut and your soul, it's personal.

Once your music is recorded, you have two options. You can either keep it to yourself, or you can release it for others to hear.

If you keep it to yourself, you are safe. It will never be criticized. You can either love it or hate it, modify it, improve it, keep it as is, or dump it, but it's your decision. It's safe in that world. It also results in nothing but satisfying yourself. If that's your goal when you set out to record, you'll have accomplished your goal, and you'll be able to sleep soundly each night.

When you release something, however, you lose all control.

You can't predict or control how people will react to what came from your soul. You may feel that what you've released is a masterpiece, and the general public may think your master-piece is junk. You may think what you've released fell short of your expectations, and the general public may love it and think it's a masterpiece. You may put years of effort into it and spend thousands of dollars on promotion that, in the end, results in the general public yawning and moving on within hours of its release. The point is, no matter how much you plan, how much of yourself you put into the project, or how great you may think it is, once you release the project, it's out of your hands. If the public digs it, great. If they don't, it stings, and it stings bad. I've felt that sting. It's no fun.

I know I'm good, damned good. I know that after forty years of doing this, I can compete with anybody in this town or any town. But I also know there are thousands of people in this region that either have no idea who I am, do know who I am but don't care, think my music is uninteresting or terrible, or think I'm pompous and overrated. I don't think I'm any of those things. I know I'm not any of those things. But as sure as I know that, I'm also sure there are people who don't like me and never will. What can I do about it? The answer is nothing, with conditions:

1. I have to have faith in my efforts: I have to know what I'm doing is good. I do.

2. I have to have faith in myself: I have to know the music I'm making is something I'll still be proud of fifty years from now. I will be.

3. I have to accept that what I do is not going to inspire or please everyone. Occasionally, I will receive criticism, sometimes harsh criticism, and sarcasm.

I'm a painting on a wall that some people think is art, and some people think is junk. Every artist is their own painting and will be judged by the general public in a variety of complimentary, apathetic, and hurtful ways.

My old Facebook friend needs to realize that he is also a painting on the wall—a painting that he decided to release for others to observe.

Either someone is going to buy the painting, or it'll be ignored. They may buy it, and it will still wind up in a garage sale, to be sold for a quarter. In the end, the artist who releases songs from his or her soul can rely on only one thing: the faith and belief in the project, which came from their own guts and soul. Is the project worthy of you? If it is, criticism won't worry you.

It's all part of the game. If you're going to play, accept the rules that go along with the game.

Did you know that Audrey Hepburn hated the color black? She actually preferred magenta. But she wore black because she knew you'd like her in black. All of us are doing things we'd prefer not to do. Suck it up people. Be like Audrey. Wear that little black dress for a while. It makes people feel better.

Italian Schooling by Neva

I was raised by a very strong Italian mother and also in large part by my big sister Debbie. I was raised beautifully and inspirationally, with an enormous amount of love from both of them, my other two older sisters, Toni and Peggy, and my younger sister, Jessica.

We lived in a house in Crystal, Minnesota. In 1966, my family purchased it for $14,000. A single mom with four kids was not met with mass acceptance in those days. Divorce wasn't as common back then. A single mom with four kids moving into this neighborhood made quite a statement, but we got through it. The house was a disaster, but we were so happy to have a home of our own, we did what we needed to do.

Mom waitressed at a place called The Point. She raised us on those finances, with little to no help from our father. She worked nights, so Debbie became our nighttime mom. She did an amazing job. The fact that we all turned out as well as we did, considering the situation we were faced with, is something that astounds me to this day.

In my early teens, a few years after we moved into that house, Mom started taking one of my friends and me to a cabin in Crosslake, Minnesota. We'd go for a week's getaway each summer. It was always a lot of fun doing that. At times, we would go to restaurants for dinner instead of eating in the cabin. One night we actually went to a nightclub to see someone she knew.

This particular night mom's friend, Jimmy Bowman, was performing. He was a Twin Cities jazz legend. I had seen Jimmy when I was a kid. He used to visit my mom and dad at the bar where they were both employed. But I had never seen him perform before. I had never seen any live performance at that time in my life, so I was in uncharted territory.

The room was full of vacationers. I could tell Jimmy was a good musician, but the music he was performing was not anything that interested me yet; I was just a kid, mind you.

I became bored, and I got distracted. I got up out of my chair and walked the few paces to a nearby jukebox. I looked at the songs for a minute or so. Then I came back to the table.

When I sat down, my Italian mother gave me a look no son wants to see. She scolded me and told me what I was doing was very rude.

She told me quite sternly and directly to never look at a jukebox while someone is performing live. She really meant it.

It didn't matter that it was her friend Jimmy—it could've been any live performer. She told me there is a certain level of respect you give someone when they're doing their job and sharing their talent. It was a huge moment in my life.

I always think of that moment when I see a live performer or a jukebox. I wish my mom had been around to share that wisdom with some of the people I have seen in live settings.

When does someone stop showing respect to a performer? What causes someone to cross the line like that?

It's different for everyone. And whether you feel disrespected, sometimes, depends on your own mood, and what you perceive the other person's intent was. I've had people assume they can grope me and more while I am singing, or later, off stage. When this happens, it can mean many things. In your teens or twenties, it could mean the sexual energy you are transmitting from stage is making people react that way.

It could be an icebreaker to a potential new relationship, or to a one-night stand. But if this happens to you when you're in your forties, and the person treating you like that is in their twenties, you become painfully aware that you may have been in this business too long.

When someone my age receives this kind of attention, it can just as easily come from a place of mockery, instead of sexual attraction. I suppose as you get older, you tend to think of the bigger picture. No one likes to be mocked. Occasionally, people want to push performers to see how much they will allow. It's a game that gets played. I stopped playing that game a long time ago. Some musicians love the game. Either way, it gets down to the idea of respect between the musician and the audience.

The main job of an artist is to entertain the audience. It is a great thing to have the ability to do that. In my book, everybody who can do it, and gets paid for it, should consider it a blessing.

But it is a job. Live musicians are doing their job. Like all businesses in day-to-day life, there is an unspoken rule of etiquette that adults are expected to know. Bands in a club are no different.

As a clubgoer, you have the choice to stay, leave, or not attend at all. Assuming you can join the band at will or seeing how far you can push a band member with your actions can be potentially embarrassing for you. What you may not realize is that your actions are most likely very embarrassing and humiliating to the musician as well.

If you need a reminder, my mom can be reached. She can bring her wooden spoon if necessary.

"Yeah, I don't run."
        —Mikaela Jensen

A Song Interrupted by Speech

The moment I held my daughter for the first time, I felt something I had never felt before. It was this undeniable, palpable sense that I was in a protection zone I had never experienced before. This adorable little girl with more hair than I had ever seen a baby born with, this girl who clearly liked it inside her mama, given how long she took to come out, was finally, beautifully, forever in my life. I was her father. I was a father to my first child. A beautiful baby girl named Mikaela M'Liss Jensen.

When I think of Mikaela and Tucker as babies, and later, in their toddler years, I often wonder . . . if Facebook had been around the late 1980s and early 1990s, how quickly would they have become viral superstars?

They were both a constant source of joy for their mama, me, and our beloved roommates, all of whom became fantastic parenting partners with us. The joy they brought was, at all times, led wonderfully, and magically, by Mikaela.

Mikaela's love for music was there from the start. The presence of music in her sphere, from the Judds to Aretha, Ray to Elton, and Springsteen to Van Morrison, fed her soul. To this day, music runs through her and seeps from her pores. It's undeniable.

When Mikaela was born, she had a slight heart defect that required attention immediately after we left the hospital. She had monthly and yearly checkups with her heart doctor, a man aptly named Dr. Wright. Thankfully the heart defect was not a significant one, but anytime there is something going on with your child's health, you are afraid of it. And we were.

During one of the visits to Children's Minnesota Hospital in the Twin Cities, Mikaela had to be scanned for nearly an hour. They wanted to see whether there was any new development with the heart issue, or if it had lessened since the last visit. This scan required her to lay still for its duration. That is a tall task for an active, happy little girl, so she was given some medication to help her relax enough to make this test possible.

This medication was supposed to take a matter of minutes to kick in. As they gave it to her, the constant array of songs that were in Mikaela's head began to flow from her cute little face. They were continuous, only interrupted by words. Then the staff shut the door and waited for her to go into a silent, peaceful state, so they could begin the scan.

As we waited in the doctor's office for this to happen, we kept hearing staff pass by the room and laugh. More and more staff members passed by and did the same.

Nearly twenty to thirty minutes after the medication was given, Mikaela was nowhere near sleepy. Her catalog of made-up songs, including her distinct version of "Three Blind Mice," where she stopped and repeated the line "See how they run" in perpetuity, was in full force. It was the laugh of the day in that office, and it is exemplary of how Mikaela, at that age and through all her days, has had a natural way of bringing joy to people around her.

A few years after Mikaela was born, Dr. Wright told us that whatever he'd heard from her heart when he first met Mikaela was no longer an issue. That was a remarkable feeling and a huge relief for her mama and me.

Mikaela, who as a baby had so much hair that at times she was mistaken for a doll, seemed evolved beyond her years: the formation of her speech, the maturity of her song patterns, and the first seeds of her humor were off the chart.

As someone who worked nights with my band, I was incredibly lucky to be able to spend as much time as I could with both of the kids during their early years.

I remember Mikaela helping me clean the floor on all fours in our first house, and her taking baths with Tucker in the kitchen sink, and later in the upstairs bathtub. At times, their friend Rosie would be at our house, and there'd be three naked children having the time of their lives, flopping around and completely soaking the bathroom floor.

There was the time when, for some odd reason, in the middle of the hottest day of summer, Mikaela announced from the top of the stairs that she was wearing her winter sledding outfit. Then she tripped and fell down a full flight of stairs, while I screamed in shock and horror.

I was able to stop her as she bounced like a ball to the second-to-last step. The child could have broken her neck or worse with this fall, but someone was watching out for her. There is no better explanation I can think of as to why she chose that time, of all times, especially on a humid summer night, to wear her snowsuit. I'm confident the suit saved her from critical injury.

My memories of this child, in those days, could fill books. But it was through those moments, those early years, that the core of Mikaela—the part all her friends, associates, and family members see to this day—was formed, solidified, and became ever constant within her.

As a child, the bond that Mikaela had with her mama and papa was quite powerful. She and Tucker clearly possessed a beautiful fifty-fifty combination of our personalities. And while it looked effortless, and certainly was joyous, we actually put thought into how we raised these two beautiful children, to make sure they felt listened to, loved, and appreciated, wherever they went. But Mikaela's deepest bond was with her little brother, Tucker. She strengthened that bond daily, from childhood through to the final moment of Tucker's life.

Long before they spoke anything resembling English, Mikaela and Tucker had a secret language only they could understand. She provided Tucker with gentle touches, and a thousand other comforts out of nowhere. Her words and touches became a protective shield she would place in front of him whenever she felt he needed it. Mikaela was the dream big sister for any little brother. I'm familiar with the role a sister can play; I had three older sisters and one younger sister. The love in my life continued to Mikaela and Tucker.

At school, from elementary through high school, Mikaela was the champion of the underdog. That has not changed one iota to this day. If you were Mikaela's friend, there was no doubt where you stood in her heart and her soul. The love she showed her friends was a continuation of the love she showed Tucker each day. It was not anywhere near the level of her relationship with Tucker, but even 10 percent of that level was more than her friends likely felt with anybody else.

She's a voracious reader, just like her mama. And like her Mama and I, she loves the theater of the absurd and a wide array of musical genres that have been in her life from the beginning. These direct lines of art, the ones we've given her, and those she's found herself, have served as the intellectual and musical centerpiece that is the essence of Mikaela.

After high school, Mikaela interned for the most successful female music promoter in the nation, Sue McLean.

Mikaela was so damned hip. Because of her past employment at Down in the Valley, a record store in Golden Valley, and her experiences with the music business, selling merch at my gigs and being on-site as a volunteer and helper at the music festivals I produced, Mikaela was a perfect fit for the office space occupied by Sue McLean & Associates.

As an intern at SMA, Mikaela had to learn all aspects of the business and be able to do all parts of the job. Her work ethic was perfectly suited to the music business, which is a business that can go smoothly or can explode into chaos in seconds. You need the ability to think fast, and you need to have some backbone; Mikaela has both.

Those attributes are plentiful in my daughter, and they served her well at SMA for all of the years she worked there. She stayed at SMA until the very sad day of Sue McLean's passing. Sue was beloved; she'd become a personal hero to me, Mikaela, and hundreds of others in this town and around the nation.

In their post-high-school years, Mikaela and Tucker's unbreakable bond seemed never-ending. Their kinship was even expressed in what, between them, became humorous.

Nobody was a bigger fan of Tucker's music than Mikaela. Nobody made Mikaela laugh more than Tucker. They were each other's go-to for multiple things in their own lives. They were at each other's side for gossip or counseling, when something happened that was hysterical or sad, and anytime something occurred in their world of friends or business activities. The bond they formed during childhood had flourished through their lives and was inexorable when we found out what was happening to Tucker.

It was a July day when we learned what was going on with Tucker. I only know what it's like to hear that kind of news as a parent; I haven't the faintest idea of what it must have been like for Mikaela.

Who knows what memories siblings as tight as the two of them share? What were they really saying to each other when we couldn't understand them? When they were little, what did their glances and looks toward each other mean? Did they mean whatever we, as witnesses, thought they meant? Or did the two of them, even then, exist with one another on a different plane, removed from what we could comprehend?

All I know is all of us were scared as hell. We laughed in those early days, but internally, we were boiling mad and so intensely sad.

There was never any doubt as to who was driving this car for Tucker. During the early days, through his treatment, it was Mikaela.

She was the point person at the Humphrey Cancer Center, the University of Minnesota Masonic Cancer Center, and the University of Minnesota hospital and ICU. She was the person who managed all of Tucker's needs, while we, his mama and papa, stood close by, loaded down with inquiries we needed to ask. But our inquiries weren't anything Mikaela hadn't already thought of. I think just as she took care of Tucker, she cared for us. She made sure there was space for us to have input as Tucker's parents.

It wasn't her throwing us a bone; she wanted our involvement because she knew we were in a pain she couldn't understand, just as we couldn't possibly, fully understand her pain. I always thought that was kind of her, actually.

It didn't hurt our feelings. We were in it.

What we were witnessing was the culmination of nearly three decades of a relationship unlike any other sibling relationship either of us, or any of our friends or family members, had ever known.

Mikaela and Tucker were again speaking a language nobody understood but them. The circumstances of those two years were unforeseeable and unimaginable. They needed that private world of theirs. They both gained strength from it.

We all spent a lot of time in waiting rooms, hospital rooms, lobbies, cafeterias, and waiting for shuttles to bring us back and forth to appointments and other locations during those years. While Tucker's mama and I certainly spent a lot of time in all of these places, we couldn't come close to the time Mikaela spent with Tucker, at the hospital, at his house, or at one of Tucker's gigs.

Anything and everything, whether it involved work or friends, was conducted in the protective and loving setting Mikaela provided to Tucker. In this way, she maximized her availability to do whatever was needed for him. What question needed to be answered? What question needed to be asked? What medication needed to be taken, and when? There were a thousand other things, too, all managed for one reason: to get Tucker through this.

The devotion of Mikaela's friends was on full display during this time, because of how she had been a champion to all of them from time to time. Many of their friends were also going through this with Tucker, and Mikaela rose to the occasion. What's even better, they rose to the occasion for Mikaela, because it was written all over her face and on every thread of her clothing: what Mikaela was feeling was at a depth her friends had no idea how to understand. We all were down there, hurting, but not like this.

Mikaela led us all through the devastating fear of losing someone we all loved. She didn't know she had that ability within her; it's something you never know until you're in the unasked-for thick of it.

How you delegate your questions? When do you need to put a particular face on, and take that face off, depending on the situation? How you share just shreds of what you're really feeling at any moment?

I proudly, sadly, and unfortunately witnessed Mikaela step up to this task, to this level of humanity, in a way that was heartbreaking and inspiring. I could not be prouder of how she did it. I'll never be sure of how she did it.

After everyone visited Tucker's room, they congregated in the waiting room and hallways for his final moments. The four of us were in the room, no friends, no extended family.

The same four who lived in the house on Penn Avenue. Then the house on Douglas Drive. The same four who rode in an old van to Grand Coulee, Washington, in the summer, who stopped at the Howdy Hotel for biscuits and gravy, and who did the thousand other things we did together as a foursome. Once again, it was just us, joined this time by the lovely nurse who administered what Tucker needed to begin this new, last phase.

Mikaela was the first one to notice Tucker had stopped breathing.

Her little brother was not in pain, nor struggling anymore, and that language between them was inexplicably, and so unfairly, interrupted in this world. Not just for them, but for all of us who had marveled at their connection and at the kind of remarkable young woman Mikaela had shown herself to be in these hard times.

How a father sees his daughter is a unique and wondrous arc. He must hold on to the relationship as tightly as he can, without applying too much pressure. And while he shares his wisdom, he must also allow her wisdom to enlighten him.

As Mikaela enters the early years of her thirties doing the job she was born to do, working at a music publishing house in Minneapolis, recommending songs for television shows and films, it's impossible not to reflect on the people and circumstances that formed this astonishing woman.

Mikaela connects to people in such a soulful way. The highs of that connection are as sweet as can be. But every joyful, strong woman has had at least one time in her life when something has brought her to her knees. That pain is so debilitating, it must seem like it's beyond the ability to recover from. But they do recover, and so will Mikaela.

There is unlimited joy and opportunity in a young girl, and it is there in the woman she becomes, the woman who is still singing her song, interrupted only by speech.

Andelse, the father smiles.

Acknowledgments

Thank you to the wonderful team at Beaver's Pond Press who met with me after a simple email to get this whole thing started. The synergy happening in that first meeting was magical and I knew full well after leaving their office I had found the right publisher, and more importantly, the right team to make this book a reality. Thank you to all of you!

Special thanks to Kerry Stapley, who read the first draft I sent and must have thought I had never attended any classes with grammar involved. Also, thank you to Hanna Kjeldbjerg, who has encouraged and supported this effort from the beginning.

Thank you to everyone who has encouraged me to write this version of my life . . . and guidance to reign in my brain at times.

Thank you to Dick Carbone for believing in my work and being so supportive of this book, the charity, and for the blessings he provided to help Tucker to go to Arizona.

Thank you to Tucker and Mikaela, who have provided me decades of the absolute best a parent could ever hope for. Your father loves you very much.

Thank you to my sisters and my amazing mother, who have always supported my interests and loved me unconditionally. I am so blessed to have all of you.

Thank you to all of the members of Mick Sterling and the Stud Brothers. Any success of that band—starting with Mark and Tim Moran in 1988 through the current lineup over thirty years later—gave me a beautiful platform to perform many different things these past three decades.

Thank you to the thousands of fans of my music the past four decades and those who have supported my varied efforts (when I have both succeeded and fallen flat on my face). I hope you feel I have never taken you for granted in any way, because I never have.

Visit **www.MickSterlingPresents.com** for upcoming events and more information about how to participate in his charities: The 30-Days Foundation and The Masterpiece Foundation (honoring his son, Tucker Sterling Jensen, by supporting cancer patients in conjunction with The Angel Foundation).

Email **Mick@MickSterlingPresents.com** for media or book club inquiries, reviews, or anything to do with his books, music, or charities.